The Wild Food Trailguide

ALAN HALL

Drawings by Katie Matthysse and Mike Firpo

Holt, Rinehart and Winston   NEW YORK

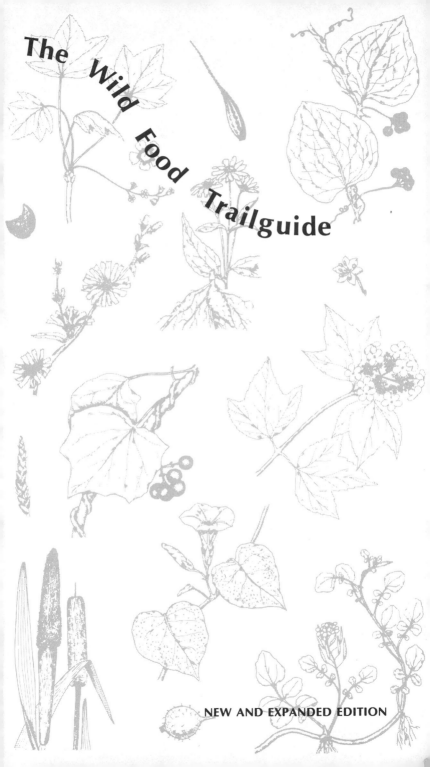

The Wild Food Trailguide

NEW AND EXPANDED EDITION

Library of Congress Cataloging in Publication Data

Hall, Alan, 1945–
  The wild food trailguide.

  Includes index.
  1. Plants, Edible—United States—Identification.
2. Food, Wild—United States—Identification. I. Title.
QK98.5.U6H34   1976   581.6'32   75–21466
ISBN 0–03–016741–8
ISBN 0–03–016746–9 pbk.

Designer: Madelaine Caldiero
Second Edition

Printed in the United States of America
10 9 8 7 6 5 4 3

Contents

Introduction

Long before man learned to hunt, harvested his first crop, or domesticated his first animal, he had collected an extensive body of plant lore. He knew what plants could be used as food and as medicine, and which would fill a number of his other needs including shelter, implements, and clothing. And even after he became a farmer, he continued to gather and use those plants that grew wild and needed no cultivation. Up to quite recent times when increasing urbanization, large-scale farming, and commercial medicines caused much wild lore to fall from common knowledge, it was a rare woodsman, farmer, or mother who lacked a familiarity with local edible and medicinal plants and their uses. Today, the number of people who regularly gather and use wild plants has dwindled, so that only the most dedicated woodsmen and the inhabitants of the more isolated rural areas keep the tradition alive, and many plants (such as Dandelion and Purslane) whose use extends back beyond man's earliest written records have come to be regarded as noxious weeds by the majority of people. Ironically, this majority spends millions of dollars yearly in frantic, fruitless, and senseless attempts at their eradication.

Fortunately, the plants are still out there growing, and as more and more people take to the outdoors, whether backpacking or canoeing into the remote wilderness or simply walking or bicycling along rural roads and amid farm country, increasing numbers are once again reaping nature's free harvest. The advent of ultralight camping gear and freeze-dried and dehydrated foods has made it possible for a man to go farther, stay out longer, and carry less than ever before, but far too often the modern camper lacks survival skills and is totally dependent on the contents of his pack. He is in a position where a simple mishap that separates him from his pack or his food supply can be a disaster ending in death. Yet even a rudimentary knowledge of the more common edible plants would enable him not only to survive, but to thrive. As Art Howe, who for 50 years was a mountain guide in the Adirondacks, once told me, "In the woods a little knowledge can go a long way . . . it can get you out alive." Possibly the greatest tragedy in the woods is the number of people who have starved to death surrounded by an abundance of food that rivals that of the markets for flavor, freshness, and nutritive value.

Even when survival is not at stake, a knowledge of wild food plants can contribute immeasurably to the enjoyment of nature; it can provide the camper with relief from boring prepackaged meals and with the gratification that he can live in the wilderness by his wits rather than by the strength of his back and the contents of his pack. The casual hiker, biker, or walker can add zest to trail lunches and anyone can add to his culinary repertoire a list of delicacies that are unavailable commercially.

But the best reason for eating wild plants is that they are just plain good. This is not to say that everyone will like everything he tries anymore than everyone likes every cultivated vegetable, but almost everyone is certain to discover a few foods he prefers to any cultivated vegetable he has tasted. In many cases, edible plants in this book are the ancestors of cultivated varieties that have been selectively bred by growers; the Wild Onion is an example. Other wild plants (Water Cress, for one) have escaped from cultivation; some (Salsify, for example) were once extensively cultivated but for inexplicable reasons fell into disuse. And still others (like Wild Rice) are of superior quality but have resisted attempts at cultivation.

In terms of nutritional value, wild plants generally come out ahead of their garden-variety relatives. In fact, a great deal of the medicinal value originally associated with many wild plants was due simply to their high vitamin content, which cured the vitamin-deficiency diseases that were so widespread in the past when green vegetables were not normally available during the winter months. These perfectly effective cures were in general use hundreds of years before vitamins were "discovered." Dandelion greens, for instance, have almost twice the vitamin A content of spinach; the young shoots of Pokeweed contain almost three times the vitamin C of oranges; and the leaves of Lamb's Quarters have three times the calcium of spinach leaves.

Learning to identify edible plants is no harder than learning to recognize other people. Like people, plants have characteristics that are similar to those found in human races, families, and individuals. With a little practice, an amateur can learn to spot specific plants in what at first looks like a confusing mass of leaves, stems, flowers, and seeds. True, there are poisonous plants, but their number is limited and, of these, very few are deadly. Perhaps most important, fewer still can be confused with edible varieties, and if care is taken in identifying the plants, all can be readily distinguished. This book is designed to enable the amateur plant hunter to make accurate and certain identifications of edible plants. The 85 plants that are covered were selected because they can be easily recognized, can supply a wide range of food products throughout the year (although the pickings are necessarily somewhat leaner in the winter months), and can be found over broad sections of the U.S. and southern Canada. These 85 plants alone provide 28 different salad greens, 18 cooked vegetables, 8 substitutes for potatoes, 18 sources of flour, 5 cooking oils and butters, 21 cold beverages, 23 substitutes for coffee and tea, and 7 sources of sugar as well as numerous potherbs, fruits, confections, jams and jellies, pies, vinegars, and even salt.

While several books are available on the subject of wild foods, all seem to me to have grave shortcomings: most fail to deal with the locating and identifying of the plants or appear to assume that their readers are trained botanists; many are just too unwieldy to take into the field. My intention in writing this book was to prepare a guide that could be easily carried and that would enable the user to make confident, correct identifications.

As important as being able to identify the plants is a knowledge of their uses. While parts of a number of cultivated vegetables are unpalatable or even poisonous, they never make it to the markets and are therefore of no consequence to most people; for example, the leaf blades of rhubarb have been responsible for a number of human deaths, while the leaf stalks are perfectly harmless. It is important for the collector of wild foods to be familiar with similar cases in uncultivated plants. Only those parts of plants designated in this book should be eaten, and only when prepared according to the information given. A good example is Marsh Marigold, which makes an excellent vegetable when cooked but is poisonous in its raw state. In most cases, the foods in this book can be prepared just like any other vegetables. Where differences do occur, they have been noted. In cases where a wild plant can provide a basic food—such as flour or sugar—that is usually purchased in its finished form, instructions for preparation are given.

This is not a cookbook and recipes have not been included. If recipes are desired, substitutions of wild foods for cultivated ones can usually be made from available recipes in any good cookbook. For more detailed recipes for many of these plants, see Euell Gibbons's several books.

The reader who wishes to extend his knowledge of wild food plants beyond the scope of this guide can refer to several other books. *Edible Wild Plants of Eastern North America* by M. L. Fernald and A. C. Kinsey (Harper & Row) provides a complete listing of the edible plants of the East and *Edible Wild Plants of the Western United States* by Donald R. Kirk (Naturegraph) provides thorough coverage of the western states. A third book, *Edible Wild Plants* by Oliver Perry Medsger (Macmillan), covers the entire U.S. but is not exhaustive.

While most of the plants in this book are abundant and in little danger of extinction, a word of caution may be in order. As man is belatedly learning, there is no such thing as an unlimited supply. Careful collection will assure an adequate supply of these plants far into the future. In many cases, digging roots will loosen the soil, thin an overly dense patch, and provide better growing conditions for the following year's crop. Collecting foliage, fruits, or seeds doesn't kill the plant. But still, take only what you need. If you see only one plant, leave it alone and next year there will be more. *Never take all the plants growing in a particular area.* Collect only those parts of the plant you intend to use so that you damage the plant as little as possible. Be considerate: many of these plants are beautiful wild flowers and appreciated for that reason. And remember, picking any plant is forbidden in most state and national parks.

I would like to thank my father, Dr. B. A. Hall, the real botanist in the family, for infecting me with his naturalist's love of the outdoors and for reading the manuscript of this book for botanical accuracy. Thanks are also due Horace Kephart who, in his lifetime, recorded with care and wit the skills of the last generations of American woodsmen in his book *Camping and Woodcraft,* and passed them on to future generations of hikers and campers. It is a tribute to Kephart that this book, originally published in 1917, is still in print. My copy, which was given to my father as a Christmas gift in 1919 and passed on to me, has traveled uncounted miles in packs and pockets.

Brooktondale, N. Y.
September 1975

How to
Locate
and Identify
Wild Foods

Edible
Wild Plants
and Their Uses

There are readily available wild plants that can provide for almost any food need short of the meat course. In this section, the plants are listed according to food use. The part of the plant that is used is enclosed in parentheses and followed by (1) the season or seasons during which the plant may be used for that purpose, and (2) the page on which the plant description appears. The information contained in these lists is repeated in the treatments of the individual plants.

SALADS

These are tender plants that can be eaten without cooking. Included here are salad greens that may be used in place of lettuce and a smaller number of roots, tubers, shoots, and stems that can be eaten raw by themselves or added to salads in the manner or radishes, cucumbers, celery, etc. Since these plants are not cooked, their nutritional value is at its maximum, particularly when they are eaten very soon after being picked. While some of these salad greens are mild, others have strong flavors ranging from peppery to bitter and are best when mixed with blander greens. It's a good idea to sample a leaf and decide how much you want to use before you begin picking. A good mild green is Purslane. Chickweed is extremely mild, in fact too mild for many tastes, but is excellent when mixed with stronger greens like Chicory or Dandelion, which are bitter, or with Water Cress or Winter Cress, which have a peppery character. Plants that grow in water that may be polluted should be disinfected before use (especially Water Cress and Cat-tail). The best method is to carry a few water purification tablets, such as Halazone, which can be bought in most camping supply stores. Mix 1 tablet with 1 pint of water, wait 30 minutes, wash the greens in the water, and rinse in fresh water to remove the chlorine taste. This treatment should be sufficient to remove any pathogenic bacteria that may be clinging to the stems or leaves.

Brooklime (leaves, stems)	Spring and summer	178
Burdock (leaves, leaf stalks, stems)	Spring and summer	192
Calamus (shoots)	Spring	48
Catbrier (shoots)	Spring and summer	56
Cat-tail (stems, sprouts)	Spring	38
Chickweed (leaves)	Spring through fall	90
Chicory (leaves)	Spring	196
Chufa (tubers)	Spring through fall	44
Cleavers (shoots)	Spring	180
Dandelion (leaves)	Spring	200
Day Lily (tubers)	All year	52
Evening Primrose (shoots)	Spring	156
Horseradish (young leaves)	Spring	110
Indian Cucumber (roots)	Spring through fall	54
Jerusalem Artichoke (tubers)	Fall through spring	188
Milkweed (shoots)	Spring	170
Mint (leaves)	Spring and summer	174
Mustard (leaves)	Spring	104
Ostrich Fern (fiddleheads)	Spring	34
Pasture Brake (young fronds)	Spring	36
Purslane (leaves)	Summer to fall	86
Sheep Sorrel (leaves)	Spring	76
Shepherd's Purse (leaves)	Spring and summer	106
Thistle (leaves)	Spring and summer	194
Violet (leaves)	Spring and early summer	154
Water Cress (leaves)	All year	108
Winter Cress (leaves)	Fall through spring	112
Wood Sorrel (leaves)	Early summer through fall	138

TRAIL NIBBLES

This group includes a few plants that are also listed under salads but that are chewed on the trail by hikers and mountain climbers. They have a moist, thirst-quenching quality and, in the case of Sheep Sorrel and Wood Sorrel, a pleasant acidity. Chewed on the trail, they alleviate that dry-mouth feeling that seems to plague walkers no matter how often they rinse their mouths out with water.

Barberry (leaves)	Spring	98
Blackberry (shoots)	Spring	128
Calamus (shoots)	Fall to spring	48
Dewberry (shoots)	Spring	128

Great Bulrush (shoots)	Fall to spring	46
Indian Cucumber (roots)	Spring through fall	54
Purslane (leaves)	Spring to fall	86
Raspberry (shoots)	Spring	128
Rose (flowers)	Summer	124
Sheep Sorrel (leaves)	Spring and summer	76
Violet (flowers)	Spring	154
Wood Sorrel (leaves)	Early summer through fall	138

POTHERBS

Potherbs are leaves that are boiled and served as greens like spinach. Since many of these plants are obtainable in the spring, identifying characteristics such as flowers and fruits have not yet appeared. For this reason, care should be taken not to include the young foliage of other nearby plants, which could be poisonous. Only small, tender young leaves should be collected; as they mature, they rapidly become tough and bitter. In the case of plants that are listed for summer and even fall, the young leaves at the top of the stems are always the most tender and mild.

The potherbs included here are listed in two groups. Those in the first group are tender and require little cooking. They should be prepared just like spinach: rinsed in cold water and boiled in the barest amount of salted water until they are tender. Don't overcook. They may be eaten as they are or with vinegar. Some potherbs have a coarse, dry texture and are improved by adding bacon during cooking or by pouring bacon fat, butter, or oil over them after draining. The potherbs requiring a minimum of cooking include:

Brooklime	Spring and summer	178
Catbrier	Spring and summer	56
Chickweed	Spring through fall	90
Cleavers	Spring	180
Coltsfoot	Spring and summer	190
Dock	Spring and summer	74
Green Amaranth	Spring	82
Horseradish	Spring	110
Lamb's Quarters	Spring and summer	80
Mallow	Spring and summer	152
Purslane	Summer to fall	86
Sheep Sorrel	Spring and summer	76

While the leaves of the plants in the second group provide good potherbs, more care in preparation is required. Some are bitter and strongly flavored; others contain poisonous substances that are soluble in the cooking water and are thrown away with it or are destroyed by cooking. Plants listed below that are not listed under salads should never be eaten raw. The difference between cooking these and the plants in the first group is that long cooking in two or more changes of water is necessary. The initial cooking waters are drained off and thrown away. To speed preparation, it's a good idea to keep a large pot of water boiling and use it to replace the first cooking water as soon as that stage is completed. Plants with tough, stringy fibers, such as Burdock, can be tenderized by adding a pinch of bicarbonate of soda to the first cooking water. While such rigorous cooking certainly doesn't improve the vitamin content any, essential and equally important minerals do remain. If not cooked in this manner, these plants are often unpalatable, but with proper preparation, they are worth the effort to the camper. They are immeasurably superior to dehydrated or freeze-dried foods.

COOKED GREEN VEGETABLES

Included here are wild plants that are cooked and served like a number of familiar garden vegetables. Young shoots are used like asparagus, several roots could be compared to turnips or beets, and other parts to green beans, peas, celery, or broccoli. As with young potherbs, those shoots that are used for food are

collected at a stage when they are extremely difficult to identify. Unless you are absolutely confident that you are getting the
right plant, don't eat it. However, many—including Ostrich
Fern and Pasture Brake—are distinctive and easily identified.

Burdock (roots, stems, leaf stalks)	Spring and summer	192
Cat-tail (sprouts, stems, flowers)	Spring and summer	38
Chufa (tubers)	Spring through fall	44
Dandelion (roots, leaves)	Spring	200
Day Lily (tubers, flowers)	All year	52
Evening Primrose (roots)	Fall through spring	156
Goat's Beard (roots, leaf crowns)	Spring through fall	198
Groundnut (seed pods)	Summer	134
Hog Peanut (seeds)	Fall to early spring	136
Japanese Knotweed (shoots)	Spring	78
Mallow (fruits)	Late spring and summer	152
Milkweed (shoots, pods, flowers)	Spring and summer	170
Ostrich Fern (fiddleheads)	Spring	34
Pasture Brake (young fronds)	Spring	36
Pokeweed (shoots)	Spring	84
Salsify (roots, leaf crowns)	Spring through fall	198
Thistle (stems, roots)	Spring through fall	194
Wild Onion (bulbs)	Spring through fall	50

POTATO SUBSTITUTES

Roots, tubers, and corms (see Glossary, p. 219) that are rich in
starch and have a mild flavor can be used as a substitute for
potatoes. All those listed here are tender and can be treated just
like potatoes: baked, boiled, fried, etc. In many cases where
root vegetables are cited, the season of availability is given as
"Fall to spring." This is because the starch is stored food for the
next year's growth and is most abundant during the winter
months. During the cold months the storage organs are usually
firm and crisp; when the plant is using the starch in the spring
and summer, it gets mushy. Developing storage organs can be
found in the summer although they are smaller and less abundant, and, as a result, more work is required to gather enough
for a meal.

Arrowhead (tubers)	Fall to spring	40
Cat-tail (roots)	Fall to spring	38
Great Bulrush (roots)	Fall to spring	46
Groundnut (tubers)	All year	134
Jerusalem Artichoke (tubers)	Fall to spring	188

FLOURS AND CEREALS

A large number of plants can be used as breadstuffs or ground into flour. While a goodly number are sufficient only for emergency use, others provide nutritious, flavorful products that can be used to prepare excellent pancakes, muffins, breads, etc.

Among the best wild flours are those prepared from nut meats. All flours require some preparation, but nut meats are among the easiest, particularly acorns. Acorns can usually be collected in great abundance, the shells are easily opened, and the meat is one large piece. And while the bitter tannin must be removed, you can let a stream or faucet do the work. Other nuts have the advantage of providing flour and cooking oils at the same time (see p. 59): smashing the nut and boiling it to separate the nut meat (which is subsequently ground into flour) from the oil and shells is often easier than picking out pieces of nut meat for immediate eating.

Those flours that are obtained from roots or tubers are probably the easiest to use in the field, and Cat-tail, Arrowhead, and Chufa are all very good in this respect. Two preparation techniques can be used. The first is best if you are preparing flour for immediate use. Free the roots of clinging mud and small rootlets and crush them with a hammer or between rocks. Then rinse them vigorously in a container of cold water to free the starchy material from the fibers. Strain out the fibers and allow the water to settle until a whitish sediment collects on the bottom and the rest of the water is fairly clear. Pour off the water, add fresh water, stir, and repeat the settling process. Repeat this until the water ceases to feel slimy. Finally, drain off all the water. The flour may be used while still wet if recipes are modified to allow for the extra liquid present. For storage or transportation, it can be dried and then ground into a powder. In the second technique, the roots are first dried, then ground into a powder, and the fibers finally sifted out.

Closer to conventional wheat flour are those prepared from wild cereals or seeds. But the similarity ends with the preparation technique; they taste very different, although they are not necessarily unpleasant. Before they can be ground into flour, the seeds must first be both threshed and winnowed. Threshing removes the husks from the seeds and winnowing separates the seeds from the husks and other trash. Some seeds have loose husks that can be freed from the seed simply by rubbing the seed between the hands, but others call for more rigorous treatment. A good way is to rub the seeds between two boards or flattened pieces of wood. Flat rocks can also be used, or the seeds can be spread on a flat surface and crushed beneath the feet. The best way to winnow grains is to pour them back and forth between two tin cans or similar containers in slowly moving air. The trash, being lighter, will blow away and the seeds will fall into the receiving can. The only real problem is the slowly moving air: if the air is moving too slowly, the trash will go right along with the seed, and if it's moving too fast, the seed will go right along with the trash. However, this method does work, and with a little practice at judging wind currents it is almost easy.

Grinding is another problem. In the field, about the only way it can be accomplished is between two rocks. The quality of the flour depends on its fineness, and no small amount of grinding is required, particularly when small, hard seeds insist on popping out from between the stones. In the home, grinding is much easier. A knife-type kitchen blender works well for small quantities and hand flour mills may be used. A good one is the Quaker City Hand Grain Grinder, which costs less than $15 and is available from Nelson and Sons (Salt Lake City, Utah).

While seeds can be used to make flour, they can also be used as cereals and boiled into mush. The only seed that is of excellent quality when boiled is Wild Rice, but many others are palatable and nourishing, which counts most in the wilderness. The addition of sugar, honey, maple syrup, or bacon fat improves them greatly. The seeds of several species are easily collected in great abundance (Dock and Lamb's Quarters, in particular) and even if it seems like too much trouble to use them for flour, they could be extremely important in an emergency.

The only source of flour that needs absolutely no preparation is the bright yellow pollen of Cat-tail, which is already finer than you could ever hope to grind it. Its extreme fineness, however, makes it exceedingly hard to wet and it is much easier to use if it is mixed with wheat flour. The baking qualities of other wild flours are often improved by blending with wheat flour and they can be used to advantage to extend dwindling supplies of flour in the wild.

Arrowhead (tubers)	Fall to spring	40
Beech (nuts)	Fall	66
Black Walnut (nuts)	Fall	58
Butternut (nuts)	Fall	58
Cat-tail (pollen, roots)	All year	38
Chufa (tubers)	Spring through fall	44
Dock (seeds)	Summer and fall	74
Great Bulrush (roots, pollen, seeds)	All year	46
Green Amaranth (seeds)	Late summer and fall	82
Hazelnut (nuts)	Fall	62
Hickory (nuts)	Fall	60
Lamb's Quarters (seeds)	Fall and winter	80
Oak (acorns)	Fall	68
Purslane (seeds)	Fall	86
Shepherd's Purse (seeds)	Fall	106
Sunflower (seeds)	Fall	188
Wild Rice (seeds)	Summer or fall	42
Yellow Pond Lily (seeds)	Fall	92

NUTS AND LARGE SEEDS

Everyone is familiar with the uses of nut meats, so little need be said here. However, acorns and sunflower seeds should be roasted before use and are not good when added to baked goods. Also, the bitterness of acorns varies from species to species and even from tree to tree, so try one out and if it's too bitter, forget it or use it for something else, like flour.

Beech (nuts)	Fall	66
Black Walnut (nuts)	Fall	58
Butternut (nuts)	Fall	58
Hazelnut (nuts)	Fall	62
Hog Peanut (seeds)	Fall to spring	136
Oak (acorns)	Fall	68
Sunflower (seeds)	Fall	188

COOKING OILS AND BUTTERS

A very limited number of North American plants have sufficient extractable oil to be worth bothering with. Still, cooking oils and butters are an important staple food, and, while early colonists relied on animal fats for this purpose, the Indians made use of the nuts and seeds listed here. One of the oils most highly valued by the Indians was extracted from the Shagbark Hickory. Oils can be extracted from nuts by crushing and then boiling them. The oil will rise to the top of the water and can be skimmed off. Skimming is easier if the liquid is poured into a narrow container; this will give the oil greater depth and reduce the likelihood of getting a lot of water mixed in with the oil.

Beech (nuts)	Fall	66
Black Walnut (nuts)	Fall	58
Butternut (nuts)	Fall	58
Hickory (nuts)	Fall	60
Sunflower (seeds)	Fall	188

FRESH FRUITS

While some wild fruits are palatable only after cooking, the vast majority can be eaten as they are picked. In the wilderness or in the absence of a freezer, wild fruits, particularly berries, can be preserved by drying. The process is simple, and dried fruits will keep for years in sealed jars. Spread the carefully washed fruit on a well-ventilated surface (a screen works very well, but a tightly stretched cloth will also work), cover with cheesecloth to keep off flies, and place in direct sunlight. Turn or stir the fruit occasionally and take it inside at night to keep dew from wetting it. The time required varies according to the moisture content and thickness of the fruit, but several days is usually sufficient. Fruit can be dried in an oven, but very low heat should be used or the fruit will cook and the flavor alter. A warm dry attic is also a good place to dry fruits. Dried fruit can be eaten as is or it can be soaked in water for a couple of hours and then used in any of the ways fresh fruit is. Herbs, such as Mint and some tea substitutes (see p. 16), can also be dried in the same manner as fruits, or bunches of stems and leaves can be hung upside down in a warm room or near the kitchen stove.

Bearberry (in an emergency)	Fall	162
Blackberry	Summer	128
Black Cherry	Late summer to early fall	130
Blueberry	Summer	164

Currant	Summer	114
Dewberry	Summer	128
Gooseberry	Summer	114
Grape	Fall	150
Ground Cherry	Late summer or fall	176
Huckleberry	Summer	164
Juneberry	Summer	118
May Apple	Late summer	96
Mountain Ash (in an emergency)	Fall and winter	116
Pawpaw	Fall	100
Persimmon	Fall and winter	168
Raspberry	Summer	128
Strawberry	Early summer	122
Wild Plum	Summer	132
Wintergreen	Fall through spring	160

JAMS AND JELLIES

The list of plants that can be used in jams and jellies is longer than that for fresh fruits because of the inclusion of several plants that are too sour to be eaten fresh, like Choke Cherry, or are slightly unwholesome when eaten raw, like Elder, but which are of excellent quality when cooked. Cases where commercial pectin is required to bring about jelling are noted in the descriptions of the individual plants. While most people prefer to make jellies at home, it is possible to make them in the wild where they can be eaten on bread or right from the pot like a confection, the sweetness and fruit combining into a welcome source of energy. Recipes for many of these conserves are on the packages of commercial pectin, and substitutions are easily made (Ground Cherry for tomato). A package of the powdered type of commercial pectin adds very little weight in a pack, although it does call for a slightly extravagant use of sugar. If less sugar is used and no pectin, the result is a sauce that makes an excellent camp dessert.

Barberry	Fall and winter	98
Blackberry	Summer	128
Black Cherry	Late summer to early fall	130
Blueberry	Summer	164
Choke Cherry	Late summer to early fall	130

Cranberry	Fall and winter	166
Currant	Summer	114
Dewberry	Summer	128
Elder	Late summer	184
Gooseberry	Summer	114
Grape	Fall	150
Ground Cherry	Late summer or fall	176
Hawthorn	Fall	120
Highbush Cranberry	Fall and winter	182
Huckleberry	Summer	164
Japanese Knotweed (stems)	Summer	78
May Apple	Late summer	96
Mountain Ash	Fall and winter	116
Raspberry	Summer	128
Rose (fruits)	Fall and Winter	124
Strawberry	Early summer	122
Violet (flowers)	Spring	154
Wild Plum	Summer	132

PIES

Fruit pies are surprisingly easy to make in camp with either a reflector oven or Dutch oven. Oil crusts are the easiest to make and require the least care. Crusts are always good (and anyway, even not-so-good things become great when prepared in primitive surroundings) although they never equal skillfully made traditional pie pastry for flakiness. All that is involved is pouring 2/3 cup of cooking oil that has been combined with about 3 tablespoons of milk over 2 cups of flour and about a teaspoonful of salt. Mix it up and roll it out. Simple fillings are nothing more than fruit combined with a couple of cups of sugar.

Barberry	Fall and winter	98
Blackberry	Summer	128
Black Cherry	Summer	130
Blueberry	Summer	164
Cranberry	Fall and winter	166
Dewberry	Summer	128
Elder	Late summer	184
Grape	Fall	150
Ground Cherry	Late summer or fall	176
Huckleberry	Summer	164
Japanese Knotweed (stems)	Summer	78
Juneberry	Summer or fall	118

Mountain Ash	Fall and winter	116
Pawpaw	Fall	100
Persimmon	Fall and winter	168
Raspberry	Summer	128
Strawberry	Early summer	122

PEMMICAN

Pemmican is a concentrated trail food that was invented by the Indians and rapidly picked up by trappers, traders, and woodsmen in the Northwest and Arctic regions. It is extremely nourishing, doesn't spoil, and a little goes a long way. As a source of sustained energy, hasty trail lunches, or survival food, it is unexcelled. And while the name "pemmican" has fallen into disuse, it is still sold to campers and hikers under the name "meat bars." But with the exorbitant prices being charged for concentrated camping and survival foods, it makes sense to make your own.

Originally the meat base of pemmican was buffalo, but beef works just as well. The beef is cut into strips and dried outdoors or in an oven until it is completely dry and crumbly. It is then ground as fine as possible, either in a meat grinder with a fine plate or by pounding. Melted suet is poured over the meat, salt is added to taste, and fresh berries are mixed in. The mixture is kneaded into a paste and packed in suitable containers—plastic tubes work well. Drying the beef reduces it to 1/6 of its fresh weight, and it is further fortified by the addition of extra fat and fruit. Pemmican can be eaten raw, boiled into a porridge, or fried like sausage. Some of the berries added to pemmican by the Indians were:

Blueberry	Summer	164
Currant	Summer	114
Gooseberry	Summer	114
Hawthorn	Fall	120
Huckleberry	Summer	164
Juneberry	Summer	118

COLD BEVERAGES

Quite a number of cold beverages can be obtained from wild plants. They range from the sweetish, watery saps of trees, to the sour, refreshing lemonade-like beverage made by soaking

Sumac berries, to the "breakfast" juices of fruits like Elder and Highbush Cranberry.

Barberry (fruits)	Fall and winter	98
Blackberry (fruits)	Summer	128
Black Cherry	Late summer to early fall	130
Black Walnut (sap)	Spring	58
Birch (sap)	Spring	64
Butternut (sap)	Spring	58
Catbrier (roots)	All year	56
Chokecherry (fruits)	Late summer to early fall	130
Chufa (tubers)	Spring to fall	44
Cranberry (fruits)	Fall and winter	166
Dewberry (fruits)	Summer	128
Elder (fruits)	Late summer	184
Grape (fruits)	Fall	150
Highbush Cranberry (fruits)	Fall and winter	182
Maple (sap)	Spring	144
May Apple (fruits)	Late summer	96
Purple Avens (roots)	All year	126
Raspberry (fruits)	Summer	128
Strawberry (fruits)	Early summer	122
Sumac (fruits)	Midsummer through early winter	140
Wood Sorrel (leaves)	Early summer through fall	138

COFFEE SUBSTITUTES

Comparatively few plants can be used as substitutes for coffee; while several have achieved wide use, they lack caffeine and fail to provide that slight "eye opening" stimulation coffee drinkers usually look forward to in the morning. Nonetheless, there are people who prefer the roasted root of Chicory to coffee and it has had a long history as a coffee adulterant. Cleavers is the only North American plant that is actually related to coffee and its flavor most closely resembles the real thing.

Beech (nuts)	Fall	66
Chicory (roots)	All year	196
Chufa (tubers)	All year	44
Cleavers (fruits)	Early summer	180

Dandelion (roots)	All year	200
Goat's Beard (roots)	All year	198
Salsify (roots)	All year	198

TEAS

Many of the plants that can be steeped in hot water and drunk as tea have had a long history of medicinal use and in some cases they do have mild medicinal properties. Others, though, owe their fame to nothing more than a pleasant flavor and several came into use during the American Revolution when Oriental tea was under embargo. One wild tea plant, Cassina, has the distinction of containing caffeine.

Birch (twigs and bark)	All year	64
Blackberry (leaves)	Summer	128
Cassina (leaves)	All year	142
Coltsfoot (leaves)	Spring and summer	190
Dewberry (leaves)	Summer	128
Elder (flowers)	Summer	184
Labrador Tea (leaves)	All year	158
Mint (leaves)	Spring and summer	174
New Jersey Tea (leaves)	Spring and summer	148
Persimmon (leaves)	Summer	168
Raspberry (leaves)	Summer	128
Rose (leaves)	Spring and summer	124
Sassafras (roots)	All year	102
Strawberry (leaves)	Summer	122
Sweet Goldenrod (leaves)	Summer and early fall	186
Wintergreen (leaves)	All year	160

WINES AND BEERS

There are few plants that have not been made into wine at some point. The list includes such unlikelies as potatoes, tomatoes, and turnips. While there are people who will swear to the quality of these dubious concoctions, those based on fruits and flowers are more suitable to less adventurous tastes. Wines made from Elder and Dandelions are well known to most people, but a fairly respectable number of wild plants make good wines. The subject of winemaking cannot be treated in a few paragraphs as some authors have attempted to do (leading to results that are seldom good enough to tempt further endeavors). While the only way to learn how to make wine is by doing it, several good introductory books are available. (One point to note: federal law requires a license; it costs $2 and allows you to make 250 gallons for private use. Write IRS and ask for Form 1541.) The wild plants covered in this book from which wine can be made are:

Blackberry (fruits)	Summer	128
Black Cherry (fruits)	Late summer to early fall	130
Choke Cherry (fruits)	Late summer to early fall	130
Currant (fruits)	Summer	114
Dandelion (flowers)	Late spring	200
Dewberry (fruits)	Summer	128
Elder (fruits, flowers)	Summer	184
Gooseberry (fruits)	Summer	114
Grape (fruits)	Fall	150
Highbush Cranberry (fruits)	Fall and winter	182
Mountain Ash (fruits)	Fall and winter	116
Raspberry (fruits)	Summer	128
Wild Plum (fruits)	Summer	132
Wintergreen (leaves)	All year	160

The flavorings of such popular carbonated beverages as birch beer and sarsaparilla were originally obtained from plants, although they are generally prepared synthetically to-day. Both of these beverages can be made at home and are every bit as good as the commercial varieties. To make them, take about 1 gallon of finely cut twigs, shaved roots, or leaves (depending on the part called for) and steep them for 1 hour in 4 gallons of boiling water. Strain off the liquid and add about 3 pounds of sugar. Place the liquid in a 5-gallon crock or other suitable container, add yeast (commercial bakers' yeast will do), cover it with a cloth, and leave it until the liquid has stopped bubbling and begins to clear. This will take about a week if it's in a warm place. Bottle it in 1-quart bottles to which 1 teaspoon of sugar syrup has been added, cap tightly, and allow it to ferment in the bottle for about ten days before drinking. This method of preparation makes a mildly alcoholic beverage. It can also be made so that it is carbonated but virtually nonalcoholic by using only 1 cup of sugar per gallon, and bottling it as soon as it begins to bubble. The plants that can be used to make beers are:

Birch (twigs and bark)	All year	64
Catbrier (roots)	All year	56
Persimmon (fruits)	Fall and winter	168
Wintergreen (leaves)	All year	160

VINEGARS

Sweet tree saps are a prime source of vinegar, although un-wanted experience with the manufacture of vinegar is often gained when homemade hard cider or wine inexplicably turns. What has happened is that it has become contaminated with a common airborne bacterium that feeds on the alcohol produced by the yeasts and turns it into acetic acid. But despite the loss of a certain quantity of alcohol, vinegar is very useful stuff in its own right. The simplest way to make your own vinegar is to start a yeast fermentation in sweet tree saps, but leave them open to the air; they are almost certain to turn to vinegar. Vinegars can also be made from any of the plants listed under wine, but less sugar should be added because sugar raises the alcohol level and when it gets high enough, the vinegar-producing bacteria can't survive.

Birch	Spring	64
Black Walnut	Spring	58
Butternut	Spring	58
Maple	Spring	144
Persimmon	Fall and winter	168

SUGARS

The best source of sugar is the Maple tree, but several other trees produce sap with a high enough sugar content to be worth boiling it down. The technique of tapping trees is briefly described under Maples (see p. 145). The roots of the Great Bulrush also contain considerable amounts of sugar. It comes nowhere near tree sugars in quality, but it is useful in a pinch.

Birch (sap)	Spring	64
Black Walnut (sap)	Spring	58
Butternut (sap)	Spring	58
Great Bulrush (roots)	Spring	46
Hickory (sap)	Spring	60
Maple (sap)	Spring	144
Persimmon (fruits)	Fall and winter	168

PICKLES

In the absence of a freezer, pickling is one of the best ways to preserve foods. Quite a bit of the vitamins and minerals leach out into the pickling liquor, but pickles are generally eaten in small quantities more for their taste and crisp texture than anything else. Any good cookbook has detailed instructions for preparing pickles. A good quick method that will let you tell if you like the result without expending a great deal of time and energy is simply to pack the prepared plant part in jars, add about 1 teaspoon of prepackaged pickling spices, fill the jars with boiling vinegar, and seal. Pickles prepared in this manner are ready to eat in four to six weeks.

Barberry (immature nuts)	Fall and winter	98
Black Walnut (immature nuts)	Summer	58
Butternut (immature nuts)	Summer	58
Cat-tail (sprouts)	Spring	38
Indian Cucumber (roots)	Spring through fall	54
Jerusalem Artichoke (tubers)	Fall to spring	188
Marsh Marigold (flower buds)	Spring	94
Pokeweed (shoots)	Spring	84
Purslane (stems)	Summer and fall	86
Wild Onion (bulblets)	Summer and fall	50

SEASONINGS AND FLAVORINGS

The seasonings and flavorings in everyday use include spices such as Mustard, herbs like bay and tarragon, and flavorings like ginger or chocolate. Wild plants provide an equally broad and varied range, many of which are familiar, some of which are not. With unfamiliar ingredients, only experimentation will tell how much to use and where to use it. A fairly good indication can be had by tasting a small quantity before adding it to other foods.

Catbrier (roots)	All year	56
Coltsfoot (leaves)	Spring and summer	190
Day Lily (flowers)	Summer	52
Elder (flowers)	Summer	184
Horseradish (roots)	All year	110
Mint (leaves)	Spring and summer	174
Mustard (seeds)	Summer	104
Purple Avens (roots)	All year	126
Rose (flowers)	Summer	124

Sassafras (leaves)	All year	102
Sheep Sorrel (leaves)	Spring and summer	76
Shepherd's Purse (seeds)	Fall	106
Wild Onion (bulbs, leaves)	Spring through fall	50

CONDIMENTS

Several wild plants can be used to prepare condiments. Sassafras root bark makes a good chutney, Ground Cherries an excellent relish, and Mustard seeds a prepared mustard comparable to that sold in the stores.

Ground Cherry (fruits)	Late summer or fall	176
Horseradish (roots)	All year	110
Mustard (seeds)	Summer	104
Sassafras (roots)	All year	102

CONFECTIONS

When chocolate had not yet become widely available, candied plants were the popular confections. The flavors of Oak, Calamus, and Wild Ginger were utilized as candies by boiling them in a sugar syrup until they were thoroughly saturated, allowing the sugar to harden, and rolling in granulated sugar to cover the sticky surface. A different kind of confection can be made from Mallow. This was the original source of marshmallow, which is now made from corn syrup, egg albumin, and starch.

Calamus (rhizome)	Spring through fall	48
Mallow (fruits and roots)	Spring and summer	152
Oak (acorns)	Fall	68
Strawberry (fruits)	Early summer	122
Violet (flowers)	Spring	154
Wild Ginger (roots)	Spring and summer	72

THICKENERS

Materials that impart body to soups, gravies, stews, etc., are important to cooking. A large number of plants have a mucilaginous quality and act as thickeners when they are cooked with other foods. For example, powdered leaves of Sassafras can be used in anything and are the equal of corn starch or flour.

Day Lily (flowers)	Summer	52
Mallow (leaves)	Spring and summer	152

Pasture Brake (young fronds)	Spring	36
Purslane (leaves)	Summer and fall	86
Sassafras (leaves)	Spring and summer	102
Sheep Sorrel (leaves)	Spring and summer	76
Violet (leaves)	Spring and early summer	154

MISCELLANEOUS FOOD USES

Several uses of wild plants do not fit in any of the previous categories and are listed here. Further details are given in the discussions that accompany the individual plants.

Catbrier (roots)	Gelatin	All year	56
Coltsfoot (leaves)	Salt	Spring and summer	190
Grape (leaves)	Food wrapping	Early summer	150
Milkweed (sap)	Chewing gum	Summer	170
Nettle (leaves)	Rennet	Spring and summer	70
Yellow Pond Lily (seeds)	Popcorn	Fall	92

Besides being edible, many of the plants included in this book have other uses that are handy for the camper or out-doorsman. In many cases, they not only contribute to a knowledge of woodcraft and to personal comfort in the wilderness, but could be important tools in a survival situation.

PLANT DYES

Colors obtained from plants were widely used by the American Indians and by early settlers and didn't fall into disuse until the development of synthetic organic colors. Some provide fast colors, but others are readily water soluble and need mordants. Boiling in a solution of alum works well with natural plant and animal fibers. In the list that follows, the colors are close approximations of those you can expect to get from the plants.

Barberry (bark, roots)	Yellow	All year	98
Black Walnut (husks)	Brown	Fall	58
Butternut (husks)	Purple	Fall	58
Catbrier (roots)	Violet	All year	56
Elder (fruits)	Purple	Fall	184
Nettle (roots)	Yellow	Spring and summer	70

New Jersey Tea (roots)	Red	All year	148
Pokeweed (fruits)	Red	Fall	84

EMERGENCY FISHBAIT

Sweet Goldenrod (galls)	Winter	186

FISHHOOKS, AWLS

Hawthorn (thorns)	All year	120

INSECTICIDE

Calamus (rhizome)	Spring through fall	48

INSULATION

Cat-tail (seeds)	Fall and winter	38

MEDICINE

Plants provide many of our most potent medicines, but in large doses they can often turn into deadly poisons. A number of plants have had long histories as home remedies and are mild enough that they can be used in the field without fear. The conditions that these plants can treat as well as some more generalized uses follow the name of the plant.

Bearberry (leaves)	Antiseptic	All year	162
Brooklime (leaves and stems)	Scurvy	Spring and summer	178
Calamus (roots)	Indigestion	All year	48
Coltsfoot (leaves)	Sore throat	Spring and summer	190
Horseradish (leaves and roots)	Diuretic	All year	110
Jewelweed (leaves)	Poison ivy, fungus infections (athlete's foot)	Spring and summer	146
Mallow (leaves, fruits, roots)	Skin lotion, sore throats, wound dressings	Spring through fall	152
Mustard (seeds)	Muscle aches	Summer	104
Sumac (fruits)	Sore throat	Midsummer to early winter	140
Violet (flowers)	Bronchial infections	Spring	154

Wild Onion (bulb)	Toothache, earache	Spring through fall	50
Wintergreen (leaves and berries)	Fever, aches and pains	All year	160

PILLOW STUFFING

Cat-tail (seeds)	Fall and winter	38

SCOURING PADS AND SOAPS

One plant—Bouncing Bet—contains a soap-like substance that can be used in the absence of soap. Horsetails are an efficient scouring pad. Another trick for cleaning greasy pans without soap is to leave them on the fire and add a little water; when it boils, throw in some ashes. The water, ashes, and grease will combine to form a weak solution of soap to clean the pan.

Bouncing Bet (leaves)	Spring through fall	212
Horsetail (stems)	Spring through fall	207

SPILES

The readily hollowed twigs of Elder can be used to make spiles for tapping sap trees.

Elder (small branches)	All year	184

STRAINERS

Cleavers (stems)	Summer	180

THREAD AND TWINE

Nettle (stems)	Spring and summer	70
Thistle (stems)	Spring through fall	194

TINDER

Cat-tail (pollen)	Summer	38
Birch (bark)	All year	64

TOBACCO SUBSTITUTES

To the smoker, there are few things worse than running out of tobacco in the woods. Two plants provide passable substitutes that can be used alone or mixed with tobacco to extend it.

How to
Use This Book

With a little care and patience anyone can learn to recognize plants. Everyone knows some of the more common plants (Dandelion, for example) and can identify them without the slightest doubt even in complete ignorance of botany. The average person, when asked to describe the shape of the leaves of a Dandelion, or their arrangement, or the structure of the flower, or the shape of the seeds, would probably be unable to do so. Yet, with unerring accuracy, he could probably identify it in a field of other plants. To him it just "looks right."

This book is designed to make it as easy as possible to identify common but less widely recognized edible wild plants. But the fact remains that it is still a book; by far the best way to learn plants is to have someone point them out in the field. In this way, you get an overall impression of the plant and it becomes as familiar and easy to spot as a Dandelion. Unfortunately, that kind of overall impression is more difficult to gain from print. With a book, you have to learn to look at plants and see their differences and similarities. Like music, in which a limited number of notes can be put together to make an almost infinite number of melodies, plants have a number of characteristics that can be arranged in an almost limitless variety of combinations. The particular combination of a relatively small number of characteristics is what makes a plant "look right." Such factors as the shape of the leaves, the arrangement of the leaves (are they paired opposite each other or do they alternate on the stems?), the color and shape of the flower, and the size of the plant add up to an arrangement that is repeated exactly in no other plant.

Botanists have arranged plants in groups based on common features. Those plants with basic similarities have been placed in large groups called families. Families are in turn divided into a number of subgroups that bear a close similarity to each other and these are called genera. Each genus is composed of a number of kinds of plants, called species, which have traits that set them apart from all other members of the genus but which also have traits in common with the other plants in the genus

25

and with the other genera that make up the family. To prevent confusing one plant with another, scientists have agreed on an international system of names, in which each plant has a first name, which identifies the genus, and a second name, which is the species. For example, the botanical name for the common Dandelion is *Taraxacum officinale*. The genus *Taraxacum* is composed of 11 species of which *officinale* is one. In turn, the *Taraxacum* genus is one of 115 genera that make up the Composite family. While a plant may have a large number of common names depending on where you find it growing and whom you ask what its name is, and while several different plants may be known by the same common name in different locales, each plant has only one scientific name.

The plants included in this book are arranged and named according to the scheme of *Gray's Manual of Botany* (American Book Company), 8th ed. It is highly technical and poorly illustrated, but considered, in botanical circles, as something of a bible. (A similar book in which each species is illustrated is *The New Britton and Brown Illustrated Flora of the Northeastern United States and Adjacent Canada* by Henry A. Gleason [New York Botanical Garden]. A version of this three-volume work is available in paperback [Dover].) By arranging the plants according to *Gray's,* it becomes easier for the reader to spot similarities between plants of the same families and genera.

The treatment of each edible plant in this book occupies two facing pages. The left-hand page contains the family name, the most widely used common names, the habitat in which the plant can be found, the seasons during which it can be used for food, the approximate size of the plant, a map shaded to show the range over which the plant grows, and a precise line drawing of the plant. The maps show the distribution in the United States, but most northern species extend into southern Canada and occasionally into Arctic regions as well. In the drawings, an attempt has been made to show the plant at the stage of growth at which it is generally used; where size and detail permit, the whole plant is shown to give an overall impression of its appearance. The right-hand page consists of a simple, nontechnical description of the plant giving those details that, in their particular combination, allow for positive identification of the plant. (A glossary of the few botanical words that could not be avoided begins on page 219.) This descriptive passage should be compared with the illustration to get an accurate impression of what the plant looks like. Following this passage is a brief description of the uses of the plant and special instructions for gathering and preparing it. At the bottom of the page, the plant parts and their uses are tabulated in chart form for easy access.

Cases where plants can be confused with poisonous species are noted, and the reader is referred to the section on poisonous plants, which begins on page 205. This section is by no means a complete list of the poisonous plants that occur in North America, but it does include those that are most easily confused with edible plants and those that are so deadly that anyone who intends to collect and eat wild plants must know them. The reader is strongly advised to familiarize himself with these plants before attempting the identification of edible ones. A good, complete book on poisonous plants is *Poisonous Plants of the United States and Canada* by John M. Kingsbury (Prentice-Hall). Dr. Kingsbury, who is a noted expert on poisonous plants, has published a smaller, less technical book on the subject, *Deadly Harvest* (Holt, Rinehart and Winston), which is available in paperback.

The procedure for locating and identifying edible plants is simple. Habitat is by far the most important single factor in locating any plant. For this reason, this chapter ends with a tabular listing of plants arranged according to habitat and including the seasons of the year during which they can be used. In these lists, the habitats are general; more specific details on habitat accompany each plant. Less fussy plants that grow in more than one habitat appear on more than one list. To use this book, first locate the table that best describes what you see around you (is it a dry open field you're in? a wet woodland trail?) and then select those plants that coincide with the season. The plants are listed in their order of appearance in the book to minimize page turning. Turn to the section on the plant you have selected. Quickly check the range map to see if you are in an area where it can be found. Then check the more detailed description of its preferred habitat and look around for likely places. Next study the illustration facing the text and check the size of the plant. Then try to spot plants of the right size that fit the description and resemble the drawing.

When you find a plant that seems to fit the description and looks like the drawing, check it carefully against both. If any characteristics don't seem to agree (leaf alignment, stem characteristics, size, etc.), don't compromise. Keep looking; you probably have the wrong plant. If all details check out, you can be confident that you have the right plant. Take a good look around and you will probably discover that you have been stepping all over them. In fact, often they'll seem to be everywhere you look and you'll wonder why you never noticed them before. This new-found ease of recognition is due to your now having an impression of the whole plant; it has joined the ranks of familiar plants.

But even though you are certain that you have the right plant, collect it carefully. Accidentally including parts of adjacent poisonous plants is probably a greater danger to the collector of wild edible plants than mistaking a poisonous plant for an edible one. When you are gathering foliage, make sure you get only the plant you want and when you are after the root, don't just dig indiscriminately around the base of the plant. Make very sure that the roots you're digging are the roots of the plant you want, particularly in aquatic habitats where the poisonous Water Hemlock may be growing. The most difficult time of year to collect plants is in the early spring when many of the identifying characteristics are not yet apparent. About the only sure way to identify young plants is by prior experience. The best approach is to learn to identify the mature plant and then look for the young ones the following year, or to keep your eyes peeled during the growing season and observe what the young plants grow into. And you don't have to be in a wilderness camp to do this. Your own backyard, an empty lot, an ordinary roadside—each is as good as place as any to start.

THE PLANTS BY BASIC HABITAT

DRY OPEN LAND

WET OPEN LAND

DRY WOODS

Edible
Wild Plants

OSTRICH FERN
Pteretis pensylvanica

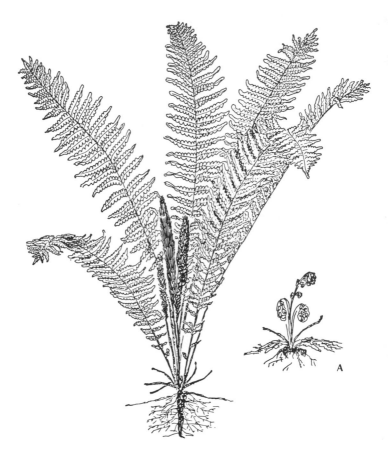

SIZE: 2–6 ft. high at maturity; collected
    when 5–6 in. high
HABITAT: Moist fertile stream banks,
    rich northern woods and slopes
SEASON: Early spring (before fronds are
    unrolled)

IDENTIFYING CHARACTERISTICS: The leaves (fronds) of this fern occur in dense clumps and look as if they'd been arranged in a vase. There are two kinds of fronds: sterile and fertile. The many sterile fronds are pinnately compound and 2–6 ft. high. Sterile frond leaflets have deeply indented edges. The central stalk of the fronds is covered with papery scales that are pale brown to cinnamon color. Leaflets vary from 4–12 in. in length and gradually become shorter toward the base of the frond. Fertile fronds are much shorter (8–24 in. high) and are found in the center of clumps of sterile fronds. Leaflets on fertile fronds are narrow and covered with rounded, pod-like fruiting bodies. The underground part of the stem (rhizome) is black, scaly, and heavily branched. In the early spring, the young fronds are frequently surrounded by the persistent, dried remains of the previous year's fronds. The young fronds (A) are commonly called "fiddleheads" because their tightly curled tops resemble the head of a violin. They have stout, rapidly tapering stalks and are covered with large, papery, brown scales.

COLLECTION AND USE: *Fiddleheads* should be collected when they are less than 5–6 in. high and the fronds are still tightly curled. Break off the fiddleheads as close to ground level as they will break freely. Two or three clusters of fiddleheads usually provide enough for a meal. The fuzz that covers the fiddleheads can be rubbed off in the hand; they should then be washed thoroughly in cold water. Take care to remove all scales including those that are in the coiled leafy tip. Ostrich Fern fiddleheads may be eaten without cooking and can be added to salads. They may also be boiled in salt water until tender. They require less cooking than Pasture Brake (see p. 36); 10 min. is usually sufficient. Cooked fiddleheads have a dry quality that can be overcome by serving with generous amounts of butter, pan drippings, or sauce. Fiddleheads take to canning well; crowns can be transplanted to wooden boxes after the fall frost and will sprout in the cellar for winter use.

Fiddleheads: salad; cooked vegetable.

PASTURE BRAKE
Pteridium aquilinum

A

SIZE: 1–3 ft. high at maturity; collected
    when 6–8 in. high
OTHER COMMON NAMES: Bracken fern,
    Hog brake
HABITAT: Pastures, dry open woods,
    and burned-over areas
SEASON: Early spring (before fronds are
    fully unrolled)

IDENTIFYING CHARACTERISTICS: Pasture Brake is the most common American fern. The part of the fern that is above ground level is really a single multiple-compound leaf that rises from an underground stem (rhizome). The leaves (fronds) rise singly from the rhizome but, since the rhizome bears a large number of leaves, the appearance is of scattered individual plants. In mature plants, the stalk of the frond rises from the ground to a height of 1–2 ft. and then splits into 3 branches. Each branch bears rows of pinnately compound leaflets in pairs that resemble birds' wings with the leaflets taking the place of feathers. Where the lower wing-shaped leaflets join the stalk there is usually a purplish nectar-producing organ. In plants that have not been disturbed or rained on recently, large droplets of sweet-tasting liquid frequently cling to the nectaries. The rhizome is about ¼ in. thick, blackish, and slightly woody in texture. It is covered with hair-like roots and branches that spread extensively under large areas of ground. Very young fronds (A) can be recognized by their proximity to the brown remains of the previous year's growth; young fronds are covered with a woolly material that can be removed by pulling the plant through a closed hand.

COLLECTION AND USE: *Young fronds* of Pasture Brake provide one of the earliest available green vegetables in spring. Only shoots less than 1 ft. high should be collected and preferably only those that do not exceed 6–8 in. Select fronds which have not yet unrolled completely, particularly ones with stouter stalks. Break off the tips as far below the curled ends as they snap off readily. When too old, the stalks become fibrous and difficult to break. Rub off the woolly covering and cook like asparagus: either in boiling salted water or by steaming. Relatively long cooking is required (30–60 min.). Young shoots have a slightly mucilaginous quality that imparts body to soups.

CAUTION: Avoid mature plants with fully opened fronds. Cases of cattle and livestock poisoning have been traced to Pasture Brake although young plants seem not to possess the poisonous principle. Also, cooking is recommended. The fern contains the enzyme thiaminase, which destroys thiamine (vitamin B_1); if sufficient quantities are eaten, B_1 deficiency results. Thiaminase is destroyed by the heat of cooking. Small quantities of Pasture Brake can safely be eaten raw in salads or as snacks, but people faced with survival in the wild should avoid it.

Young fronds: cooked vegetable; thickener; salad.

CAT-TAIL
Typha latifolia;
   also *T. angustifolia,*
   T. glauca, and
   T. domingensis

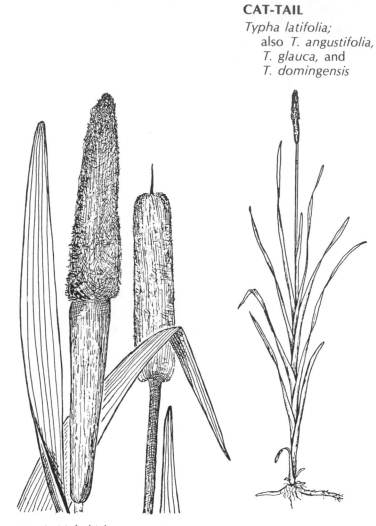

SIZE: 3–12 ft. high at maturity

OTHER COMMON NAMES: Cat-o'-nine-tail,
   Flag, Reed mace, Cossack
   asparagus

HABITAT: Shallow water of marshes and
   streams, margins of ponds and
   lakes; some species in brackish
   water

SEASON: Spring, stems and sprouts;
   summer, flowers and pollen; fall
   through early spring, roots

IDENTIFYING CHARACTERISTICS: Aquatic plants that often reach 10 ft. in height, Cat-tails' most obvious feature is the cigar-shaped flower spike that occurs at the top of a long stalk extending upward through a cluster of pale green, tape-like leaves. These leaves wrap around and tightly sheathe the stalk toward its base and often extend below the surface of the water. The flower spike is actually a great many minute flowers. Before flowering it is green; as it develops it turns brown, starting at the bottom and spreading upward. Later it is covered with loose yellow pollen; in the fall it releases a cottony mass of windborne seeds, some of which often cling to the spike throughout the winter. The leaves are ¼–1 in. wide and taper gradually to a point; veins are parallel and run the length of the leaves. In the spring the young leaves look like sword blades when they first appear above water level. The roots are rope-like, branch frequently, and are ½–1 in. thick. (*T. latifolia* is illustrated.)

COLLECTION AND USE: The Cat-tail is a year-round food source. In the spring when young leaves are 1–2 ft. high, collect young *stems* by pulling upward on the clusters of young leaves. The stems readily break free of the roots. Peel the leaves away to expose a crisp, white core up to 18 in. long. It can be eaten raw in salads or boiled like asparagus. Still-green immature *flower spikes* can be eaten as a cooked vegetable. Remove their papery husk, boil in salted water for a few minutes, and eat like corn on the cob. Since spikes reach maturity over a 6-week period, they can be eaten through much of the summer. The yellow *pollen* on older spikes provides a source of flour during the same period. It is extremely abundant and easily collected by rubbing spikes through the hand over an open container. Although pollen can be used by itself, it resists wetting and is easier to handle if mixed with equal parts of wheat flour. The *roots* are rich in starch and can also be used as a source of highly nutritious flour from late fall until leaves appear in the early spring. Flour can be prepared by drying peeled roots, pulverizing the core, and sifting out the fibers. Another way is to crush the peeled roots in water, strain out the fibers, and allow the starchy material to settle through several changes of water. Flour can be dried and stored or used in its wet state. Enlarged areas at the leading ends of roots that form the sprouts of the next season's leaves have a starchy core that can be collected from fall to early spring and eaten raw in salads or cooked as a substitute for potatoes. In early spring, the *sprouts* together with the bulb like en largement can be boiled and eaten or pickled in vinegar. The Cat-tail has nonfood uses as well. The *leaves* are the source of rush material for chair seats. (Collect when still green and hang in bundles to dry; to use, soak in water until soft.) The *cottony seeds* are good for pillow stuffing and insulation. Dry pollen makes excellent tinder.

Stems: salad; cooked vegetable. *Flowers:* cooked vegetable. *Pollen:* flour; tinder. *Roots:* flour; potato substitute. *Sprouts:* salad; cooked vegetable; pickle. *Leaves:* rush mats. *Cottony seeds:* pillow stuffing; insulation.

ARROWHEAD

Sagittaria; many species,
particularly *S. latifolia* and
S. cuneata

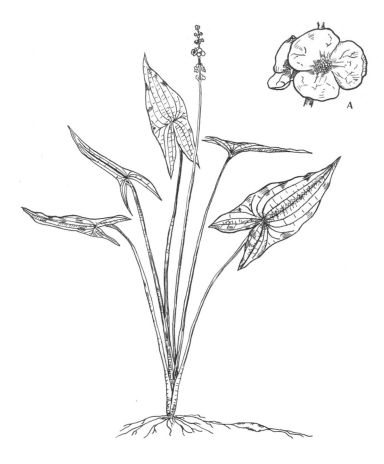

A

SIZE: 1–2 ft. high

OTHER COMMON NAMES: Swamp potato,
Duck potato, Katniss, Wapato,
Tule potato

HABITAT: Shallow waters of ponds,
swamps, and streams having rich
mud bottoms; fresh to brackish
waters

SEASON: Fall to spring

IDENTIFYING CHARACTERISTICS: This aquatic plant gets its name from the shape of its leaves, which are distinctly 3-lobed and rise directly from the rootstock. After fall frosts, their brown stalks can frequently be spotted protruding above the surface of the water. Flowers are borne on a single naked stalk that often extends well above the tops of the leaves. The flowers (A) are delicate, white, and have 3 filmy petals. They usually occur in whorls of 3 arranged around the flower stalk. Late in the season, rounded heads composed of flat seeds form near the top of the flower stalk, frequently in groups of 3. The roots are fine and fibrous and spring directly from the base of the clumps of leaves; no solid, deep-penetrating rootstock is present. At varying distances along the roots, the roots enlarge to form tubers that are pure white and have a smooth texture inside. (*S. latifolia* is illustrated.)

COLLECTION AND USE: The round *tubers* of the Arrowhead range from pea size to 1–2 in. in diameter. They were a staple food of the American Indian and related species are cultivated in China. The tubers form at distances of up to 5 ft. from the parent plant in late summer or early autumn and may be collected thereafter throughout the winter in regions where waters remain unfrozen. Since the tubers float, collection is relatively easy. The Indians dug around in the mud with their bare feet and collected the tubers as they floated to the surface, but rakes, camp shovels, and stout sticks can also be used with good results. The tubers contain a milky juice that has a bitter flavor which is destroyed by heat—after cooking they have an agreeable sweetish taste. They can be prepared in any of the ways potatoes are cooked including frying, baking, boiling, or roasting. Dried tubers can be ground into flour.

Tubers: potato substitute; flour.

WILD RICE
Zizania aquatica

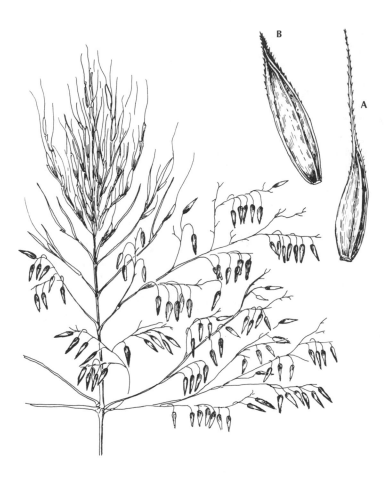

SIZE: 4–6 ft. high but can go to 10 ft.

OTHER COMMON NAMES: Water rice,
Indian rice, Water oats

HABITAT: Still shallow water of ponds,
lakes, and river mouths with rich
mud bottoms; fresh to brackish
waters

SEASON: Midsummer to early fall, when
ripe

IDENTIFYING CHARACTERISTICS: Wild Rice is a large aquatic grass that is found at low altitudes over most of its range but is particularly abundant in the Great Lakes and upper Mississippi regions. The leaves are lance-shaped with blades that are 1–2 in. wide and 1–3 ft. long. They are flat, have parallel veins, and occur alternately along the stalk. The lower portions of the leaves form long sheaths around the stalk. The stalks bear 2 types of flower clusters. At the top of the stalk is the seed-bearing or pistillate cluster. It is erect, many-branched, and resembles a broom. The seeds are dark purple and are covered with husks that have bristles at their tips (A). Several inches below the pistillate clusters are the staminate, or pollen-bearing, cluster. The staminate cluster is composed of many side branches of the stalk, each of which also branches several times. Each branch is tipped with a purplish flower (B). The staminate cluster is more open and feathery than the pistillate cluster.

COLLECTION AND USE: Wild Rice can be collected effectively during the very few days when it is ripe enough to separate freely but before the *seeds* drop of their own accord. The harvesting method used by the Indians is still the best. A canoe or open boat is paddled among the rice plants, the seed heads are pulled over the boat, and the grain is knocked free by rapping with a stick. After harvesting, the seed should be dried thoroughly either indoors or in the sun. Before use, the grain should be parched in a shallow pan over a slow fire or in a slow oven, stirring constantly to avoid burning. When the rice has cooled, rub the grains through the hands to break up the husks and then winnow to remove the chaff. The grain has a smoky flavor that can be removed by washing in cold water before cooking. Cook like rice. (The grains expand in volume 2–3 times during cooking.) Use as a breakfast cereal or with meat. It also makes an excellent thickener for soups and can be ground into a flour.

Seeds: cereal; flour.

CHUFA
Cyperus esculentus

A

SIZE: 8–24 in. high

OTHER COMMON NAMES: Nut grass,
    Earth almond

HABITAT: Damp, but not swampy,
    sandy soil; sometimes in cultivated
    ground

SEASON: Spring through fall

IDENTIFYING CHARACTERISTICS: Chufa is a sedge with a triangular stem that grows to a height of about 2 ft. and is surrounded by a cluster of tape-like leaves of almost equal height that all originate at ground level. They are pale green, from ¼–½ in. wide, and have a prominent midrib. The stem is topped by another cluster of 3–9 smaller leaves that curve up around a golden brown flower cluster. The flower cluster resembles an inverted umbrella. It has several short erect ribs and from 2–9 longer spreading ones that are up to 4 in. long. The ribs have numerous short lateral branches that are all arranged in the same plane and are covered with numerous tiny golden-brown flowers (A). The branches of the ribs sometimes have branches that in turn bear the smaller flower-covered branches. The overall appearance of the flower cluster is feathery. Long horizontal roots run out from the base of the plant and are terminated by round tubers ¼–½ in. in diameter.

COLLECTION AND USE: This plant is cultivated for its nut-like *tubers* in many parts of the world and its history as a food plant has been a long one. Chufa tubers have been found in ancient Egyptian tombs. The runners that bear tubers are easily broken, so careful collection is required. The tubers are fairly easy to collect in loose, sandy soil (which the plant prefers anyway) but where plants are found in harder soils the tubers are usually small and form far from the parent plant. In the right soil conditions, tubers will form in profusion and close to the base of the plant. The tubers have a sweetish nut-like taste and contain a milky juice. They can be eaten fresh or boiled as a vegetable. If they are thoroughly dried over a slow fire or in an oven, they can be ground into a flour that is one of the best wild flours available in North America. Chufa that has been roasted to a dark brown and ground makes a coffee-like hot beverage. A cold drink popular in Spain is made by soaking Chufa in water for 2 days and then mashing it in fresh water and sugar and straining out the solids. Dried tubers will keep almost indefinitely.

Tubers: salad; cooked vegetable; coffee substitute; beverage; flour.

GREAT BULRUSH
Scirpus validus; also *S. acutus*

A

SIZE: 3–6 ft. high
OTHER COMMON NAMES: Tule, Mat rush,
   Soft-stem bulrush
HABITAT: In shallow brackish or fresh
   waters of ponds and marshes
SEASON: Fall through early spring, roots;
   fall to spring, young shoots;
   summer and fall, pollen, seeds

IDENTIFYING CHARACTERISTICS: Bulrushes have tall naked stems that are usually several feet high. The soft, easily compressed stems are light green, pithy, and have circular cross sections. Leaves are long and tape-like, remaining tightly wrapped around the stems over much, or all, of their length to form a sheath. Flowers are in elongated spike-like clusters which are either solitary or in groups just below the tip of the stem where they hang from short branching stems. The rhizome (underground stem) runs parallel to the surface of the ground and is reddish, stout, and scaly. The tiny hard fruits (A) are nearly flat but have slightly convex sides and are surrounded by 6 bristles that attach at the bottom of the fruit and extend slightly above it at the top. (*S. validus* is illustrated.)

COLLECTION AND USE: The *root* of the Bulrush is rich in starch and sugar and was held in high repute by the American Indians. The rootstock can be dug in the fall and early spring. It can be eaten like potatoes by roasting for 2–3 hrs. or it can be cut into pieces and added to stews, soups, etc. Before cooking, root hairs and outer rind should be scraped or peeled off. A nourishing and sweet-tasting flour can be prepared by drying the roots, pounding them, and sifting out the fibers. Flour can also be made by boiling the roots into a gruel and removing the fibers. The resulting product can be dried to a white powder or used in its wet state for pancakes and bread. The younger and smaller roots are very rich in sugar and can be used to make a syrup by first bruising them and then boiling them down (for a long time) in water until the desired thickness is reached. The syrup can then be poured off the fibrous, starchy residue. In the fall, the young leading tip of the root that will put forth the next year's *shoots* is crisp and tender and can be eaten raw to relieve thirst and provide sugar. *Seeds* are available from after flowering until winter and can be ground and cooked into a mush or parched and eaten like nuts. The *pollen* is also edible and was pressed into cakes and baked by Indians. The leaves have also been used as a source of rush (see Cat-tail, p. 38).

Root: flour; sugar; potato substitute. *Shoots:* trail nibble. *Seeds:* flour; cereal. *Pollen:* flour. *Leaves:* rush.

CALAMUS
Acorus calamus

SIZE: 2–5 ft. high at maturity
OTHER COMMON NAMES: Sweet flag,
    Flagroot, Sweet rush
HABITAT: Swamps; pond and river
    margins; wet places
SEASON: Spring

IDENTIFYING CHARACTERISTICS: Calamus has sword-shaped leaves that are up to 3 ft. long and look rather like Iris leaves. The yellow-green leaves rise directly from a horizontal rhizome. Where they join the rhizome just below the surface of the water they are often purplish-red. The flowers are supported by a stalk that resembles a modified leaf. The minute flowers are borne on a finger-like spike that projects at an angle from the stalk 1–2 ft. below the top. The rhizome has numerous roots along its length and is covered with the papery remains of the bases of old leaves. All parts of the plant give off an aromatic and somewhat gingery fragrance when bruised.

COLLECTION AND USE: In the early spring the center of the *young shoots* is composed of a number of immature leaves that make a fragrant addition to salads or can be eaten in the field. They may also be added to soups and stews as a seasoning. The *rhizome* was once used as a confection. Collect the smaller parts of the rhizome, which will tend to be the most tender (but still pretty tough), wash them, and peel off the outer rind. Cut into small pieces and boil in many changes of water until soft. This takes about 8 hr.; unless the water is changed frequently the finished candy will have too strong a flavor to be palatable. Finally boil for an additional 15–20 min. in water with enough sugar added to make a heavy syrup. Drain and let dry. Powder produced by drying and grinding the *roots* is a natural insecticide. The powder has also been used as a remedy for numerous ills including indigestion and heartburn.

CAUTION: Avoid confusion with Wild Iris or Blue Flag (*Iris prismatica,* see p. 211), which can cause severe digestive upset. The Wild Iris is generally smaller (rarely exceeding 3 ft.), bears the familiar Iris flower on a single naked stalk, and lacks the aromatic smell characteristic of Calamus.

Young shoots: salad; trail nibble. *Rhizome:* confection. *Roots:* insecticide; medicine.

WILD GARLIC, WILD ONION, WILD LEEK, CHIVE
Allium; numerous species

A

SIZE: Leaves 6–12 in. high; flower stalk
    1–2 ft. high
HABITAT: Meadows, rich woods, and
    gravelly stream banks
SEASON: Spring through late autumn

IDENTIFYING CHARACTERISTICS: The first indication of the presence of members of the *Allium* genus is often the characteristic onion odor, which is particularly strong around plants that have been stepped on. They all have underground bulbs that can either be solitary or occur in groups. Bulbs of most species are small; the largest are those of Wild Leek, which are 1–2 in. long. Most have soft, narrow leaves; only the Wild Leek *(A. trioccum)* has broad leaves, 1–3 in. wide. Flowers range from greenish-white to pink and are borne in an umbel (a type of flower cluster that looks like an upside-down umbrella) at the top of a naked stalk. In some species the leaves shrivel before flowers appear (notably *A. trioccum*). The flowers of several species, including Wild Garlic *(A. canadense),* are few or absent; instead, the flower stalk bears a cluster of small bulblets (A) that are arranged like the cloves in a head of cultivated garlic. The Wild Onion *(A. cernuum)* is also known as the Nodding Onion because the umbels are bent over and hang down rather than being held erect as in other species. Chives *(A. schoenoprasum)* have very narrow, hollow, cylindrical leaves and pink flowers that are in a dense, round cluster. One species, Field Garlic *(A. vineale),* has an exceptionally strong and persistent flavor and is generally not eaten. (*A. canadense* is illustrated.)

COLLECTION AND USE: All species of this genus are edible and can be prepared in any of the ways onions are, but the wide variation in flavor and strength makes it wise to taste a small amount before deciding whether to use it as a cooked vegetable or a seasoning. Collect *bulbs* in early spring or fall when they are moist and fleshy. They can be boiled and eaten as a vegetable. In the more strongly flavored species a second change of water may be desirable. In the spring, bulbs with the tender inner leaves still attached can also be cooked by boiling. The clusters of *bulblets* that appear on flower stalks of some species, particularly *A. canadense,* make an excellent vinegar pickle. They usually are present in May or June. The young *leaves* of most species are tender and may be used as seasonings in salads, soups, etc. The best are those of the Chive. Members of the *Allium* genus have also been widely used as medicines. Garlic was a common stomach remedy. Bulbs have been placed in the ear to cure earaches, against teeth for toothaches, and the juice of the bulb has been used in wound dressings.

CAUTION: If the onion smell is missing, don't try the plant. It could be Fly Poison or Death Camass (see pp. 208 and 209).

Bulbs: cooked vegetable; seasoning; medicine. *Bulblets:* seasoning; pickle. *Leaves:* seasoning.

DAY LILY
Hemerocallis fulva
and *H. flava*

SIZE: 2–3 ft. high
HABITAT: Roadsides, edges of fields, and
    old homesites
SEASON: Summer, flowers; spring
    through fall, tubers

IDENTIFYING CHARACTERISTICS: This is a plant that has escaped from cultivation and now grows wild over a large section of North America. It gets its name from the fact that its flowers open for one day and then wilt; each plant bears numerous flowers that open over a period of several weeks. The flowers are borne on a densely branching, naked stalk. They are large (about 4 in. long) and funnel-shaped. The flowers of *H. fulva* are a tawny orange color; those of *H. flava* are yellow, smaller, and have a fragrant smell. Leaves are ½–1 in. wide and are long and tape-like, rising directly from the top of the rootstock. They have a heavy central ridge, or keel. The roots are fleshy and fibrous and form small elongated tubers in clusters directly under the plant. The plant spreads rapidly and often forms dense patches.

COLLECTION AND USE: Unopened flower buds, opened *flowers,* and withered flowers may be eaten. Unopened buds boiled in salted water for a very few minutes make an excellent cooked vegetable. Buds and opened flowers can be dipped in batter and fried like fritters. Both open and withered or dried flowers can be added to soups and stews, where they provide body and impart an interesting flavor. The flavor of dried and freshly collected flowers is somewhat different and they should be tried both ways. If flowers are dried for later use they should be soaked until soft in cold water before using. The softened dried flowers will have a slightly gelatinous quality. The small *tubers* can be dug anytime during the period when the ground is unfrozen. Only firm, young tubers should be collected. After digging they should be washed clean of clinging earth and freed of small rootlets. Boiled in salted water they have a flavor reminiscent of sweet corn. They can be eaten raw as a salad and are sweet and crisp with a pleasant nutty flavor.

Flowers: cooked vegetable; flavoring; thickener. *Tubers:* cooked vegetable; salad.

INDIAN CUCUMBER
Medeola virginiana

A

SIZE: 1–2 ft. high
HABITAT: Rich woodland soil
SEASON: Spring through fall

IDENTIFYING CHARACTERISTICS: The distinctive appearance of this forest plant places it among the more easily recognized wild food plants. It has a single, unbranched stem that is ringed by a whorl of leaves about halfway up and topped by another whorl of smaller leaves. The lower whorl has between 5 and 9 leaves that are lance-shaped and pointed at each end. The leaves lack leafstalks and are from 2–5 in. long. The terminal whorl usually consists of 3 leaves. They are smaller (1–2 in. long) and are more oval in shape than the lower leaves. The shiny green leaves have prominent parallel veins along their lengths. When the plants first come up in the spring, they are covered with loose wool which soon disappears although some may remain around the bases of the leaves. Indian Cucumber flowers in May or June. There are between 3 and 9 flowers that are borne on long, drooping flower stalks in a cluster that rises from the center of the top leaves. The flowers are about ½ in. across and have a greenish-yellow color. The flower has 6 petal-like segments (3 sepals and 3 petals) and 6 stamens. The fruits (A) are dark purple berries having few seeds. The root is a horizontal white tuber ranging from 1–3 in. long and about ½ in. in diameter.

COLLECTION AND USE: There is very little evidence that Indians ever actually ate Indian Cucumbers but the name of this plant is at least half accurate: it does taste a lot like cucumber. The crisp, starchy *root* is easily collected anytime during the growing season. The roots are near the surface and are usually found in soft soil or loam. They make an excellent snack in the wild where their moist, crisp texture and cucumber taste can be very refreshing. Simply wash off the clinging earth and peel the root. With the addition of dressing they make a fine salad or addition to salad greens. The roots can be preserved by pickling and the result is very good.

Root: trail nibble; salad; pickle.

CATBRIER
Smilax; about 12 species

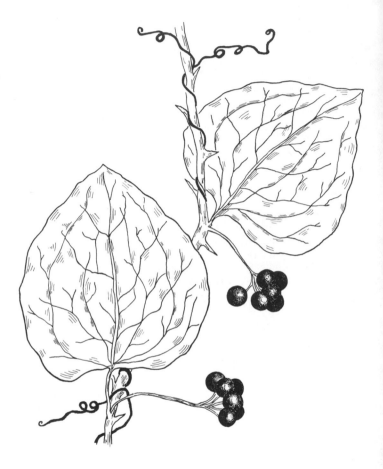

SIZE: Vines climbing on woodland brush and trees

OTHER COMMON NAMES: Greenbrier, Bullbrier, Sawbrier

HABITAT: Species in rich damp woods, swampy woods and bogs, open dry woods, dry-to-moist sand dunes, and waste areas

SEASON: Late spring and summer, young shoots; all year, roots

IDENTIFYING CHARACTERISTICS: These perennial climbing vines are chiefly southern and subtropical plants although some species extend into southern Canada and one, *S. californica,* occurs in southern Oregon and California. Catbriers are easily recognized by the thorns on their stems and by their tendrils, which twine around the plants on which they are climbing. The stems are slender and green (even in winter) but are usually woody, particularly near the base. They branch frequently and form dense tangled masses. The stems of most species have stiff, sharp thorns; only *S. tamnoides* has few thorns and they are weak and usually found only at the bases of the stems. The tendrils occur in pairs at the bases of the leafstalks and look very much like the tendrils on grape vines. The leaves of all species have a curious double vein pattern. One set of veins runs longitudinally parallel to the midrib of the leaf. The other forms a branching, net-like pattern covering the entire leaf. The more common species can be distinguished by their leaves: the most widely distributed species, *S. rotundifolia* has broad, rounded or heart-shaped leaves; *S. tamnoides, S. glauca,* and *S. Bona-nox* are fiddle-shaped but *S. tamnoides* has nearly thornless stems and *S. glauca* leaves have white undersides; *S. laurifolia* leaves are oblong with bluntly pointed tips and are evergreen and leathery when mature; the leaves of *S. californica* are broad and heart-shaped. The rootstocks of *S. tamnoides* and *S. Bona-nox* have fibrous tubers. (*S. rotundifolia* is illustrated.)

COLLECTION AND USE: The young *shoots* and branches of all species can be used as a salad green or a potherb. They can be collected from spring into late summer but become less common as growth begins to slow with the onset of fall. The leaves, stems, and tendrils can also be used but only as far back on the branch as they are most crisp and tender and can be easily pinched off with the fingers. As a potherb, very little cooking is required. The *roots* of Catbriers contain a substitute for gelatin. The tuberous roots of *S. tamnoides* and *S. Bona-nox* are best for this purpose. They should be crushed by pounding and then washed in water. Allow the sediment to settle, pour off the water, and let the sediment dry. The result is a fine red powder. About ⅛ cup of this powder boiled in 1 pint of water and cooled will form a reddish jelly with a bland taste reminiscent of sarsaparilla. The powder mixed with flour can be used to make pancakes or added to soups and stews as a thickener; it can also be mixed with hot water and sugar, cooled, and used as a beverage. The roots of other species do not release sufficient gelatin, but chopped, boiled, and mixed with sugar, they produce a flavored liquid; boiled with Sassafras root bark (see p. 103), sugar, and yeast, and allowed to ferment in the bottle, they make a good root beer.

Shoots: salad; potherb. *Roots:* gelatin; beverage; beer; flavoring.

BLACK WALNUT AND BUTTERNUT
Juglans nigra and *J. cinerea*

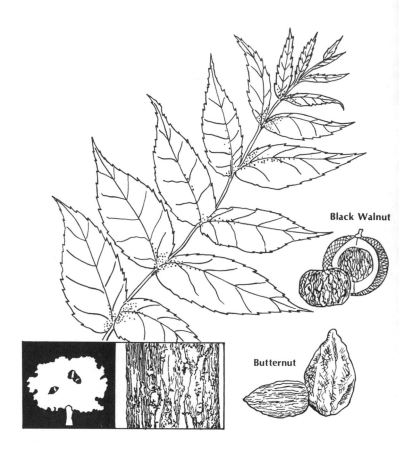

Black Walnut

Butternut

SIZE: Trees, up to 75 ft. high
HABITAT: Rich woods
SEASON: Summer, fall

IDENTIFYING CHARACTERISTICS: These are tall, nut-bearing trees that have large, alternate, pinnately compound leaves. The leaflets are lance-shaped with serrated edges and may number as many as 17. The fruits are covered with a thick, green, fleshy, and fibrous husk that is tightly bonded to the nut. When the husk is removed, the exposed nutshell is blackish-brown with a deeply furrowed, rough surface. The bark of the trees is also rough and furrowed. The Black Walnut is the more abundant of the two. Its fruits are spherical, 1–2 in. in diameter, and have smooth surfaces. The lower surfaces of the leaflets are covered with downy hairs. Butternut is sometimes known as White Walnut because of its similar but lighter colored wood. It is limited to the northeastern part of the range and seldom is found south of Georgia and Arkansas. It bears pointed elliptical fruits that are covered with sticky hairs. The fruits are ½–1½ in. in diameter and 1–2 in. long. The bark of the Butternut is lighter colored than that of Black Walnut, being almost gray while that of Black Walnut is dark brown.

COLLECTION AND USE: Because these trees are highly prized for their wood, they are becoming scarce in many parts of their range. A single tree produces an abundance of *nuts*. When the nuts are still on the trees in the summer and before they get too hard to be cut in half with a knife, they may be pickled. To prepare for pickling, plunge entire immature nuts into boiling water, then rub free of hairs. Further boiling softens the nuts and removes the bitter tannin. Change water often; when it stays fairly clear, pack nuts in jars with vinegar and pickling spices. In the fall, collect mature nuts from the ground. The fresh *husks* contain a strong dye that is almost impossible to remove, so wear gloves. The husk can be removed in the field but it is easier to get off if the nuts are allowed to dry first. Then papery dried husks are easily pulled off and will not stain the hands. The dye from the husks is readily extracted into water by boiling; Black Walnut produces a rich brown and Butternut a purple color. These are tough nuts to crack— smashing with a hammer or rock is about the only way to get the meat out—but the flavor of the nut is excellent, particularly in baking. Oil or nut butter can be prepared by smashing the husked nuts, then boiling slowly in water. The oil and nut meats will rise to the top and can be skimmed off while the pieces of shell will settle to the bottom. The oil can be separated from the nut meats, which may then be dried and used as flour; or the nut meats can be mashed into the oil (or use a blender) to produce a rich nut butter. The *sap* of these trees can also be tapped in the early spring and used as a beverage or boiled down for syrup or sugar in the same manner as that of the Maple (see p. 145). It can also be fermented into vinegar (see p. 18).

Nuts: pickles; oil; flour; nutmeat. *Husks:* dye. *Sap:* sugar; beverage; vinegar.

HICKORY
Carya; several species

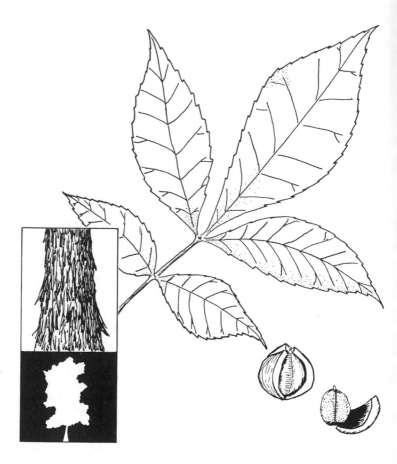

SIZE: Trees, 40–60 ft. high
HABITAT: Rich woods and bottomland
SEASON: Fall

IDENTIFYING CHARACTERISTICS: Like the Walnut or *Juglans* species, members of the *Carya* genus have alternate, pinnately compound leaves with lance-shaped leaflets that have serrated edges. However, the leaves are smaller, usually having less than 9 leaflets. The uppermost 3 leaflets are often larger than those lower down; the terminal leaflet is often the largest. The fruits are distinguished from the *Juglans* by being smaller (½–1½ in. long) and by having husks that split into 4 sections when the nuts mature rather than remaining tightly attached. The nutshell is smooth and bony. The best nut tree of the *Carya* genus is the Shellbark or Shagbark Hickory *(C. ovata),* the source of the nuts sold commercially. The tree's distinctive gray bark splits into long shards that cling loosely to the trunk. Its leaves are composed of 5 leaflets, the terminal one ranging from 4–8 in. long and 2–4 in. wide. The shell is whitish-brown. Mockernut *(C. tomentosa)* nuts are as good as those of *C. ovata* but the reddish-brown shells are extremely tough to crack and removal of nutmeats is tedious. (Mockernut is a corruption of the Dutch "Moker noot" or heavy hammer nut.) Leaves of the Mockernut tree have 5–9 leaflets and the bark is deeply furrowed but does not split free as in Shagbark. The nuts of the Sweet Pignut *(C. glabra)* are usually good but vary and some have a tendency to be acrid. Its leaves have 5 leaflets; the terminal is the largest, ranging from 3–7 in. long and 1–2¼ in. wide. The husk on the fruit is dark brown and smooth and breaks free less easily than those of *C. ovata.* The nuts of the Bitternut or Pignut *(C. cordiformis)* are quite bitter. Leaflets range from 5–9; the husk splits only to below the middle; the nutshell is heart-shaped and gray. The *Carya* genus also includes the Pecan *(C. illinoensis),* which occurs in the wild only in the southern Mississippi basin. *(C. ovata* is illustrated.)

COLLECTION AND USE: Hickory *nuts* can be gathered from the ground in late fall. They generally drop after almost all the leaves have fallen. Husks are easily pulled free and often are knocked loose when the nut hits the ground. For eating raw, roasting, cooking, and baking, the Shagbark or Shellbark is the best. The tougher shelled and less tasty nuts can be used to make flour, oil, or nut butter in the same manner as the *Juglans* species (see p. 59). In early spring, the Hickory trees can also be tapped for *sap,* which can be used as a beverage, boiled down for syrup or sugar, or fermented for vinegar (see p. 145).

Nuts: nutmeat; oil; flour. *Sap:* sugar; vinegar.

HAZELNUT
Corylus americana and *C. cornuta*

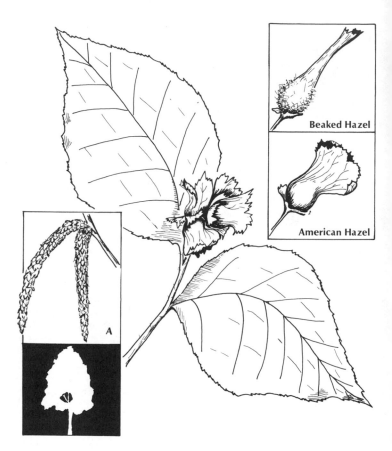

Beaked Hazel

American Hazel

A

SIZE: Large shrubs, up to 10 ft. high
OTHER COMMON NAMES: Hazel, Filbert
HABITAT: Thickets, fields, and clearings;
    borders of woods
SEASON: Late summer and early fall

IDENTIFYING CHARACTERISTICS: Hazelnut bushes grow in dense clumps that are easily spotted in the early spring when they display slender, 3–4 in. long catkins (A) that appear before the leaves. The leaves are alternate and simple, with a short leafstalk. They are oval with rounded bases and sharply pointed tips; the edges of leaves have fine teeth. The American Hazelnut *(Corylus americana)* bears nuts that are covered by a loose husk that hangs open at the end and has a fringed appearance. The nut itself is usually about 1 in. long, brown, and has a thin, bony shell. *C. americana* is limited to the eastern U.S. and is concentrated in the South; the northern boundary of its range extends from Maine to Saskatchewan. The Beaked Hazelnut *(C. cornuta)* is less common in the South, where it is limited to mountainous areas, but extends north across Canada to British Columbia and south in the western mountains through Oregon, Colorado, and into California. Although Beaked Hazelnut bushes are slightly smaller than those of the American Hazelnut, the most striking difference is in the husk that covers the nut. The husk of *C. cornuta* extends well beyond the end of the nut and forms a tubular beak that is about 1–1½ in. long. It is covered with stiff bristles and has a fringed appearance at the end. The nutshell is a pale whitish-brown.

COLLECTION AND USE: The *nuts* of both species are of excellent quality and closely resemble the European hazelnut or filbert. They ripen in late summer and will remain clinging to the bushes until they are collected or removed by squirrels and chipmunks. The nutmeats can be eaten like commercially available filberts or ground into a meal either by pounding or in a hand mill. The meal can be used in place of flour to make excellent cakes.

Nuts: nutmeat; flour.

BLACK BIRCH, YELLOW BIRCH, WHITE BIRCH
Betula lenta, B. lutea, and *B. papyrifera*

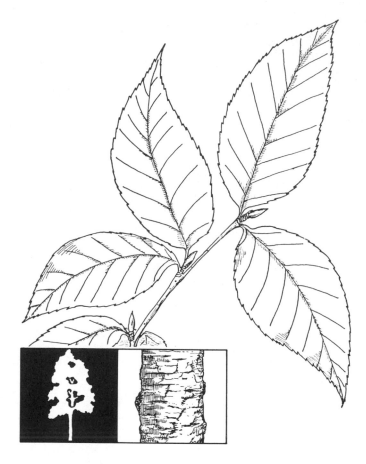

SIZE: Trees, 30–80 ft. high
HABITAT: Rich, moist woods
SEASON: All year, twigs; spring, sap

IDENTIFYING CHARACTERISTICS: Black Birch *(B. lenta)* and Yellow Birch *(B. lutea)* are found in relatively limited ranges in the eastern U.S. Black Birch is found throughout the Appalachians, from mountainous areas of Georgia and Tennessee northward to Maine and New York. The southern boundary of the range is the same for Yellow Birch but it extends further north into southern Canada and westward to Iowa. Together they are known as the Sweet Birches because the bark and leaves contain an aromatic oil with the smell of wintergreen. The most positive means of identification is the smell of a crushed leaf or twig. The leaves are oval and come to a sharp point at the tip, while the bases are rounded or heart-shaped. They have 8 or more pairs of veins that are indented into the upper surface. The edges of the leaves are finely toothed. The bark of the Black Birch, which is also known as Sweet Birch or Cherry Birch, is dark brown, resembles the bark of cherry trees, and, on young branches and twigs, is covered with small dots that look like pores. Yellow Birch bark is yellowish-to-silvery-gray and irregular pieces loosen, giving the tree a shaggy look. The White, Paper, or Canoe Birch *(B. papyrifera)* has a wider and more northern range: from Labrador to Alaska and southward into the northern states and the mountainous areas of California. It does not have the wintergreen aroma; the leaves are less pointed and have 7 or fewer pairs of veins that are raised above the surface of the leaves rather than being impressed. The bark is white, although sometimes tinged with pink or brown, and it separates easily into thin, papery layers.

COLLECTION AND USE: All 3 Birches are copious producers of *sap*. This is tapped in the same way as Maples (see p. 145) but it reaches its peak later, usually in April. The sap can be used as a beverage as it comes from the tree or boiled down to a syrup or sugar. While Birch sap contains only about half the sugar of Maple sap, it flows much faster. Birch beer can be made by combining sap with sugar or honey, boiling for about an hour, cooling, and adding yeast. Another method is to steep young *twigs* of the Sweet Birches in boiling water, add sugar (3 pounds to 5 gallons of liquid), cool, and add yeast. Sap can be made into vinegar by adding yeast. Young twigs and fresh or dried inner *bark* of Sweet Birches can be used to make wintergreen tea. The inner bark can be ground into flour and has been used as an emergency or survival food. The bark of the White Birch is useful in making camp containers and is a superb source of tinder. It is extremely resinous and will, when soaking wet, burn with a hot enough flame to dry out and ignite small twigs.

Sap: beverage; tea; sugar; vinegar. *Twigs:* tea; beer. *Bark:* beer; tinder.

BEECH
Fagus grandifolia

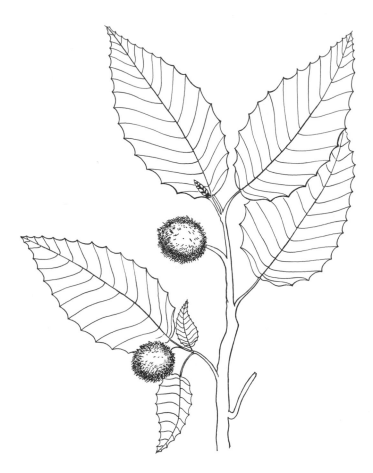

SIZE: Large forest tree, up to 100 ft.
high
HABITAT: Rich uplands and bottomlands
SEASON: Fall

IDENTIFYING CHARACTERISTICS: Beech is a tall forest tree that frequently grows with Oak and Maple in American deciduous forests. It has smooth, light gray bark that is firmly attached and may have faint horizontal lines upon close examination. The leaves are quite thin and are a pale yellowish-green; in the fall they turn a pale coppery-yellow and have a soft papery feel. They have triangular bases and curve up to a sharp point, tend to be about twice as long as they are wide, and have sharply toothed edges with a straight vein running into each tooth. They alternate on the branches and attach by short leafstalks. The trees bear both fertile and infertile flowers. The sterile, or staminate, flowers are in ball-like clusters that hang from long stems; the fertile, or pistillate, flowers occur in pairs at the end of a short stalk that attaches to the branch at the base of an upper leaf. The fertile flowers mature into a bur that is covered by soft, recurved spines and splits into four distinct sections as it turns brown and ripens in the fall. The bur contains two triangular nuts, each of which contains one sweet seed, or nutmeat. The burs are about ½ in. in diameter.

COLLECTION AND USE: Probably because of their small size, beechnuts are rarely collected today and consequently they rank as one of the great neglected delicacies of the American woods. These sweet little *nuts* have a fine flavor and are rich in oil (they were commonly used to prepare table oil in Europe during the last century). Nor are they that difficult to collect—in a Beech forest the nuts can be gathered by the bushel. The only real problem is beating out the squirrels and numerous birds that have no preconceived notions about their size. While the trees usually have too much straight, unbranched trunk to make climbing practical, a sheet of plastic or a blanket laid on the ground when the ripe nuts are dropping will produce a bounty. And unlike some of the wild nuts that have tough, thick shells, beechnuts can be pried open with a fingernail. Besides being of excellent quality fresh, the nuts can be made into flour or used as a source of oil. To make flour, simply mash the nutmeats, let the resulting paste dry out, and grind. About 1/6 of the weight of the nuts is oil that can be removed by pressing after mashing the nuts into a paste or by boiling and skimming the oil off the top of the cooled liquid. This oil improves with storage and should periodically be drawn off the top of the waxy, mucilaginous sediment that will form. The roasted nuts when ground can be used as a substitute for coffee.

Nuts: nutmeat; flour; oil; coffee substitute.

OAK
Quercus; numerous species

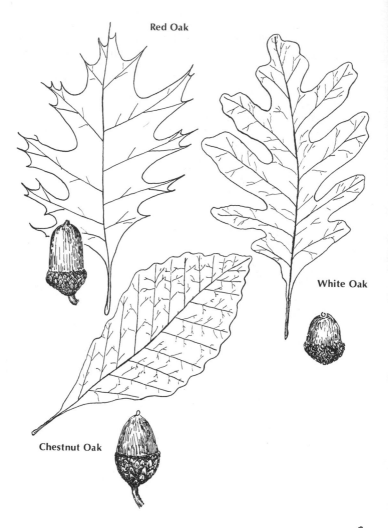

Red Oak

White Oak

Chestnut Oak

SIZE: Trees, up to 75 ft. high
HABITAT: Woods—wet and dry, rich
    and sterile
SEASON: Early fall

IDENTIFYING CHARACTERISTICS: Oaks are easiest recognized by their fruits—acorns. While the various species in this large genus range from shrubs to large trees and show wide variation in leaf shape and bark, all bear the characteristic acorn. Acorns consist of a smooth, pointed, thin-shelled nut (usually oval but sometimes more rounded) that fits into a rough cup-like cap. The cap is topped by a woody stem that attaches the acorn to the tree. The Oaks are divided into 2 groups: the White Oaks and the Red or Black Oaks. Since the acorns of the White Oaks are sweet, they are generally preferred for food purposes over those of the Red Oaks, which contain large amounts of tannin and are often very bitter. The 2 groups are readily distinguished. The first group —which includes the well-known eastern White Oak *(Quercus alba)* as well as the Post Oak, Burr Oak, Chestnut Oaks, and Live Oak—has leaves that are oval to oblong and are divided into a number of large, irregular lobes in most species although the Chestnut Oaks have rounded teeth and Live Oak has smooth edges, and both lack lobes. The bark of trees in the White Oak group is usually scaly and the inside of the nutshell is smooth. The leaves of the Red Oak group (including the Red Oak [*Q. rubra*] along with Pin Oak, Black Oak, Yellow Oak, and Jack Oak) have bristles at the tips of the lobes of those having lobed leaves and at the tips of the leaves of those lacking lobes. The bark of the Red Oak is not shaggy; the nutshells have downy linings.

COLLECTION AND USE: *Acorns* can be collected in the early autumn when they fall from the trees although hoards collected by squirrels the preceding season and forgotten can sometimes be found in hollow trees at other times of year. Acorns from the White Oak group can be roasted over a slow fire or in an oven and eaten as nuts but since all acorns contain some tannin, which imparts bitterness, they are best used after further preparation has removed the tannin. Tannin is readily soluble in water and can be removed by leaching. Whole nutmeats can be freed of tannin by boiling in repeated changes of water until the water ceases to turn brown. They can then be dried by roasting and either eaten as nuts or boiled in sugar syrup for a confection. The major use of acorns is as a source of flour, and it was once a staple food of many American Indian tribes. To prepare acorn flour, shelled nutmeats are allowed to dry, then ground into a meal and the tannin leached out. Leaching can be accomplished by placing the meal in a cloth bag or a porous container and pouring boiling water over it, or by the slower method of immersing in running cold water for several days. In the wilderness, the easiest method is to place the bag of meal in a creek or spring and forget it for several days. After leaching, allow the flour to dry in the sun or a slow oven. It cakes when drying, making a second grinding necessary before use. It can be pressed into cakes before drying to make storage and transport easier. The resulting flour is best when blended with either cornmeal or wheat flour. Pancakes, bread, and muffins prepared from it are a rich black and have a pleasant, rather nutty, flavor.

Acorns: nutmeat; flour; confection.

NETTLE

Urtica gracilis;
  also *U. dioica* and others

SIZE: 1–3 ft. high
HABITAT: Bottomlands, rich woods,
  waste areas, and roadsides
SEASON: Spring and summer

IDENTIFYING CHARACTERISTICS: The stems, leafstalks, and undersides of the leaves of these plants are covered with fine, hair-like bristles that, when they touch the skin, cause a painful stinging sensation lasting about 10 min. In fact, the generic name of the Nettles is derived from the Latin *uro,* to burn. Plants are usually erect and somewhat stout in appearance and have oval-to-oblong leaves with coarsely toothed edges and pointed tips. The leaves are dark green, have many prominent veins, and are arranged in pairs opposite each other along the main stem of the plant. In late summer, Nettles bear tiny, greenish flowers on branching clusters that originate where the leafstalks join the stem of the plant. (*U. dioica,* Stinging Nettle, is illustrated.)

COLLECTION AND USE: While most people's initial reaction on coming in contact with this easily identified plant is to avoid it, they are depriving themselves of an excellent potherb that is at its best in the spring but can also be used throughout the summer. The stinging element is instantly destroyed by boiling in water but up until that point wearing gloves to handle Nettles should not be thought of as a sign of cowardice. In the early spring, *young shoots* and *leaves* can be used, but as the season advances all but the young leaves still opening at the top of the plant become too tough to eat. They can be prepared by boiling in salted water; they also make an excellent addition to soups. Nettles can be used to prepare a substitute for rennet by boiling leaves in water to make a strong "tea" that is then mixed with salt in the ratio of 2 parts of salt to every 3 of nettle tea. One or 2 teaspoons is usually sufficient to convert 1 quart of warm milk (powdered milk will work) into rennet pudding or junket. These plants also have nonfood uses. A yellow dye can be prepared by boiling the *roots.* Mature *stems* have a fibrous layer that can be peeled free and divided into individual fibers that are extremely strong. They can be used as an emergency source of thread or twisted together to make twine. Nettle fibers were once woven into cloth in Scotland.

Young shoots: potherb. *Leaves:* potherb; rennet. *Roots:* dye. *Stems:* thread.

WILD GINGER
Asarum canadense

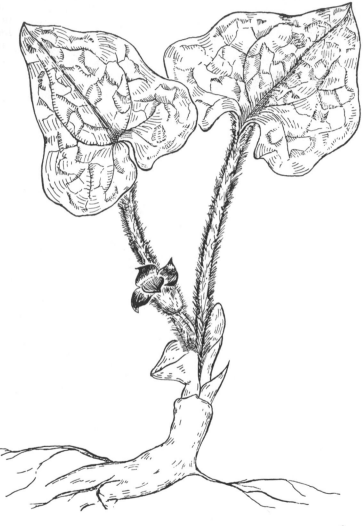

SIZE: 6–10 in. high
OTHER COMMON NAME: Asarabacca
HABITAT: Rich woodland soil,
    particularly in limestone regions
SEASON: Spring and summer

IDENTIFYING CHARACTERISTICS: The most common Wild Ginger (*A. canadense*) is found throughout the North as far west as Minnesota. Several other species with more limited ranges grow in the wooded, mountainous parts of the Northwest extending south into California. Wild Ginger plants have long, creeping, branched rhizomes that run horizontally just below the surface of the ground. The plant has only 2 leaves but usually grows in close proximity to a number of others, which makes it easier to spot. The twin leaves are on long leafstalks that rise directly from the ground. They are broad and heart-shaped with a short, abrupt point at their tips and are from 3–6 in. wide. At their bases, they are deeply indented where the 6–10 in. long leafstalk attaches to the blade of the leaf. Both the leaf blades and the stalks are covered with soft hairs, which give the leaves a gray-green, woolly appearance. A single reddish-brown flower appears in late spring. It is borne on a short stalk that originates between the leafstalks at ground level. The flower is about 1 in. in diameter. It is tubular toward the base but spreads into 3 petal-like pointed lobes at the top. (*A. canadense* is illustrated.)

COLLECTION AND USE: While it is not related to the commercially available ginger root of Asia, the pungent *roots* of *Asarum* can be substituted for the other with equally good results. Because they are horizontal and close to the surface, the roots are easy to dig; hands or a flat stone are usually sufficient. They can be dug anytime during the growing season. The long slender roots can be cut into thin slices and used in Chinese cooking, either in their fresh state or after drying. Since they are not quite as pungent as commercial ginger, slightly more generous use of Wild Ginger is recommended. The dried root can also be ground and used as flavoring in salad vinegars or mixed with pickling spices. A confection can be prepared by boiling the roots first in water and then in a thick sugar syrup in which they are left to sit for several days before removing and rolling in granulated sugar. Besides providing a pleasant candy, it is said to soothe sore throats and has been used as a remedy for stomach disorders.

Roots: flavoring; confection; medicine.

DOCK
Rumex crispus;
  also *R. patientia* and others

SIZE: 8–60 in. high
HABITAT: Waste areas, fields, and
    roadsides; some species in swamps
SEASON: Spring and summer, leaves;
    summer and fall, seeds

IDENTIFYING CHARACTERISTICS: A total of 16 species of the *Rumex* genus are known as Docks and all are edible. The Docks are stout, dark green plants having oblong to lance-shaped leaves. The largest and most prominent leaves are borne at ground level; those leaves situated alternately further up the stem of the plant are smaller. The leaves at the base are frequently 6–12 in. long and have rather stout, tapering leafstalks that are covered with a papery and slightly slimy membrane where they join the stem. Flowers are tiny and range from green to purplish-green. They are borne in tightly packed whorls along the upper part of the stem. After flowering, the upper part of the stem is covered with numerous fruits (A) that consist of a single seed surrounded by thin, papery membranes that look like wings. One of the best Docks for food purposes is the Yellow or Curled Dock *(R. crispus)*. It is easily distinguished from the other species because its leaves have very wavy or curled edges. Another, the Patience Dock *(R. patientia),* was once cultivated in Europe as a garden plant. It is one of the largest Docks and sometimes reaches 5 ft. in height with leaves that can be 2 ft. long. The Bitter, Blunt Leaved, or Red Veined Dock *(R. obtusifolius)* is suitable for early greens but rapidly gets very bitter in early summer. It is usually 2–5 ft. tall, has red veins in the leaves and stems, and broad leaves that are heart-shaped at the base rather than narrowing as in the other Docks. (*R. crispus* is illustrated.)

COLLECTION AND USE: The young *leaves* of all the Docks are too bitter to make a salad green but cooked they are an excellent potherb. Even so, most people prefer to cook in 2 changes of water. Leaves of most species remain tender enough for use until flowers are formed in the summer, and they lose little bulk in cooking so it is not necessary to collect great quantities to make a meal. Docks are closely related to Buckwheat and some species produce large quantities of *seeds* that are readily collected and can be ground into flour or, in an emergency, boiled into a mush. Seeds can be collected by pulling the stem through the hand over a suitable container. The husks should be broken free from the seeds and winnowed out before grinding into flour (see p. 9).

CAUTION: Don't confuse these plants with the Burdocks *(Arctium)* which have different uses (see p. 192). While they do look quite like the Burdocks, the latter lack sheathing membranes where the leaves join the stem and have leaves with velvety undersides; Dock leaves are smooth on both sides.

Leaves: potherb. *Seeds:* flour; cereal.

SHEEP SORREL
Rumex acetosella; also *R. acetosa*

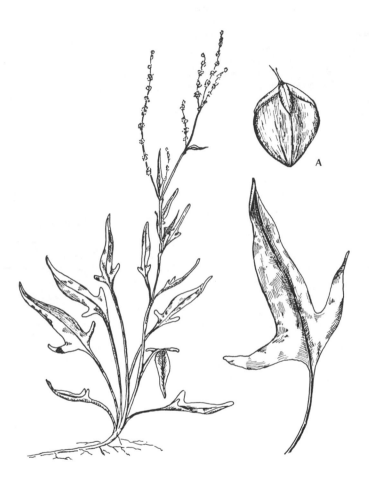

SIZE: 8–12 in. high
HABITAT: Worn-out fields and waste
    areas; in sour soil
SEASON: Spring and summer

IDENTIFYING CHARACTERISTICS: The Sorrels are similar to the Docks, being members of the same genus, but are generally smaller (see p. 74). The Sheep Sorrel *(R. acetosella)* has soft-textured, pale-green leaves that are arrowhead in shape but the lower lobes point strongly outward and the central lobe is slender and lance-shaped. Flowers are bright red and are borne in dense whorls on branches at the upper end of the stem. Red pigment sometimes also colors the leaves. The seeds (A) look much like those of Dock but the 3 wing-like membranes are smaller and only obvious at the top of the seed. The roots are long and slender. The Garden, or French, Sorrel *(R. acetosa)* is cultivated in Europe as a salad plant but has become widely distributed in North America. It is a larger, stouter plant that rises from a taproot. Its leaves are also shaped like arrowheads but the central lobe is broader than that of Sheep Sorrel and the 2 lower lobes point more backward than outward. The stems and leaves of all species contain a sour juice. (Don't let the name of this plant mislead you into confusing it with the Wood Sorrels of the *Oxalis* genus [see p. 138].) *(R. acetosella* is illustrated.)

COLLECTION AND USE: The young *leaves* of the Sorrels have an acid, astringent quality that makes them excellent in salads when mixed with other greens. The leaves have a thirst-quenching effect when chewed in the field. Boiled, they make a delicious potherb that is available until the plants flower. A refreshing drink similar to lemonade can be prepared by steeping the leaves in hot water, sweetening with sugar, and cooling. A liquor prepared by boiling the leaves of *R. acetosa* in water can be used like rennet to convert milk to pudding or junket. The leaves can be added to soups and stews for a thickener and can be used as a seasoning for fish, potatoes, etc.

Leaves: salad; trail nibble; potherb; beverage; rennet; thickener; seasoning.

JAPANESE KNOTWEED
Polygonum cuspidatum;
also *P. sachalinense*

OTHER COMMON NAME: Mexican
    bamboo
SIZE: 4–12 ft. high at maturity
HABITAT: Abandoned homesites and old
    gardens, waste areas, and
    roadsides
SEASON: Spring to early summer

IDENTIFYING CHARACTERISTICS: These are large perennial plants that propagate by underground stems, or rhizomes, and grow in dense, rapidly spreading clumps. Native to Japan and eastern Asia, they were introduced to Europe and North America as decorative plants but rapidly spread into the wild. Their most distinctive feature is their hollow stems, which resemble bamboo and are divided into jointed sections; the joints, or nodes, are swollen and each is covered by a papery membrane that looks like a cuff. The stems of Japanese Knotweed *(P. cuspidatum)* are a mottled green and look as if they have been lightly dusted with fine white powder. The leaves are about 6 in. long and are arranged alternately on the stem. They have prominent leafstalks and the blades are basically round in shape but are flattened at the base and come to an abrupt point at the tip. Elongated clusters of small greenish-white flowers are borne at the junctures of the leaves and the stems, mostly toward the top of the plant. Giant Knotweed *(P. sachalinense)* is similar but larger; its stems are coarser and marked with a series of fine parallel lines along their lengths; its leaves are longer (12 in.) and come to a more gradual point. (*P. cuspidatum* is illustrated.)

COLLECTION AND USE: The young *shoots* of Japanese Knotweed are eaten before they leaf out. At this stage they resemble asparagus and can be recognized by the presence of papery dried stems of the previous year's growth, which persist through the winter. Shoots up to 1 ft. high, before the leaves begin to unroll, can be cooked in boiling water or steamed to make a fine cooked vegetable. They are very tender and require little cooking. They can also be cooked and eaten cold as a salad. Because Japanese Knotweed contains a considerable amount of acid, it has a tartness that commends it to the same uses as rhubarb. The *young stems* up to 2–3 ft. high can be used in sauces, jams, and pies. Stems that have long sections should be selected. The sections are separated and the fibrous outer layer peeled off. Care should be taken not to peel too deeply as the walls of the stems are thin. When cut into thin crosswise sections, the stems can be boiled with sugar to make a very good sauce or used as the basis for a tart, green jam (with commercial pectin), or pie filling.

Shoots: cooked vegetable. *Young stems:* jam; pies.

LAMB'S QUARTERS
Chenopodium album

A

SIZE: 8–48 in. high

OTHER COMMON NAMES: Pigweed,
     Goosefoot

HABITAT: Cultivated fields and waste
     areas with rich soil

SEASON: Spring into summer, leaves; fall
     and early winter, seeds

IDENTIFYING CHARACTERISTICS: This is an erect, many-branched plant having leaves that are coated with a slightly waxy white powder that is more pronounced on the undersides. Because of this powder covering, the leaves are water repellent; if wetted, water either runs off or forms beads. The pale green leaves are 1–4 in. long and have long leafstalks. They are arranged alternately on the stems and are shaped rather like the feet of geese, being broad and somewhat triangular at the base and then narrowing toward the tip in a series of blunt, almost wavy, teeth. Older plants bear tiny green flowers crowded in small spikes interspersed with the leaves. After flowering, the spikes are covered with small dull black seeds (A) that are almost flat and have convex faces.

COLLECTION AND USE: Lamb's Quarters *leaves* make an excellent potherb that is considered by many people to be superior to spinach. And like spinach, it loses a great deal of bulk in cooking so an ample supply should be collected. Young plants are best, but this plant continues to put up new shoots that can be used well into summer. The leaves are not bitter, and the cooking water need not be changed. *Seeds* can be collected by rubbing them from the spikes into an appropriate container. They are available from the time they are dry in the fall until they drop, often well into winter. The seeds are extremely abundant and it is often possible to gather several quarts in less than an hour. Winnow out the husks and trash, and then grind the seed into flour. Since the seeds are very hard, grinding can be difficult: the seeds slip away from the grinders in hand mills (although kitchen blenders work well). To get around this, it helps to boil them until they are soft, then mash up the softened seeds and allow them to dry out before grinding. The flour produced from the seeds is very black. It is good for making pancakes, muffins, etc., and can be used by itself or mixed with wheat flour. The mush produced by boiling seeds until they are soft can be eaten as a breakfast cereal or emergency food.

Leaves: potherb. *Seeds:* flour; cereal.

GREEN AMARANTH
Amaranthus retroflexus
and related species

SIZE: 1–4 ft. high
OTHER COMMON NAMES: Pigweed, Wild
   beet
HABITAT: Waste areas, fields, and
   cultivated ground
SEASON: Spring and summer, leaves;
   late summer to fall, seeds

IDENTIFYING CHARACTERISTICS: The Amaranths bear a strong resemblance to the plants of the *Chenopodium* genus (see p. 80) and both are also known as Pigweed in many locales. However, the two groups are easily told apart. The leaves and stems of the Amaranths are covered with hairs whereas those of *Chenopodium* are smooth and covered with powder. Also, the Amaranths have very prominent veins. *Amaranthus retroflexus* is the species that is most frequently used for food although about 10 similar species can also be used. The leaves of *A. retroflexus* are lance-shaped with long leafstalks and have smooth edges. They are arranged alternately on coarse, rarely branching stems. In late summer, small greenish flowers are borne on elongated, branching spikes at the top of the plant; in the fall, the flowers are replaced by dense clusters of small, shiny black seeds. The root, and sometimes the bottom of the stem, is reddish.

COLLECTION AND USE: *Young leaves* can be used as a potherb until the plants flower in late summer; at that point, they become too bitter for most tastes. They should be boiled until tender (generally about 20 min.). In the fall, the *seeds* can be collected and ground into flour. The easiest way is to gather the entire spike and free the seed by rubbing it between the hands over a cloth or a plastic sheet. Vigorous rubbing will free the seeds from the husks, and the trash can then be threshed out. The dark flour made by grinding the seeds can be used to make pancakes, muffins, etc., or can be boiled into mush. While Amaranth flour was used by several Indian tribes, it has a rather musty flavor and is improved by mixing with wheat flour or cornmeal. In an emergency, the seeds can be eaten raw, boiled into mush, or added to meat dishes to provide bulk.

Young leaves: potherb. *Seeds:* flour; cereal.

POKEWEED
Phytolacca americana

A

SIZE: Up to 10 ft. high at maturity
OTHER COMMON NAMES: Poke, Scoke,
    Garget, Pigeonberry, Inkberry
HABITAT: Rich soil of cultivated areas,
    new clearings, and roadsides
SEASON: Spring

IDENTIFYING CHARACTERISTICS: This is a stout, rather rank perennial plant with smooth stems that become a rich purple at maturity. Leaves are lance-shaped to oval with smooth wavy edges. They are arranged alternately on the stem, have long leafstalks, and often reach 6–10 in. in length. Flowers are greenish-white and are borne along 4–6 in. long stalks that rise from the stem opposite the leaves. In the fall, flowers are replaced by berries of such dark purple that they appear almost black. The berries are filled with a crimson juice. The plant rises from a taproot that in old plants can be enormous, sometimes reaching several feet in length and being 4–6 in. in diameter. The taproot contains a strong purgative once used as a medicine but which should be treated as poisonous. In the spring, the shoots (A) are best recognized by the presence of the persistent remains of the previous year's growth.

COLLECTION AND USE: Despite its slightly unpleasant description, Poke-weed is probably the most widely used wild vegetable in North America and has been introduced into Europe, where it is cultivated. In the spring, *young shoots* less than 6 in. high make an excellent cooked vegetable. They should be cut off at ground level with care taken to avoid getting any of the root, which is poisonous and has a bitter taste. If the shoots show any purple coloration, avoid them; also avoid mature stems, which are somewhat poisonous. Shoots can be prepared like asparagus. The partly opened *young leaves* can be treated like spinach. Cooking in 2 waters is recommended and long cooking (up to ½ hr.) is often necessary before they are tender enough to eat. Peeled young shoots are also good when fried in batter or cornmeal and they can be made into pickles by first blanching and then covering with hot vinegar and pickling spices. A winter supply of Pokeweed shoots can be obtained by digging the large roots after the first killing frosts in the fall, cutting them back to 6–8 in. lengths, and planting in deep boxes of earth in the cellar. They will put forth strong new shoots that can be harvested over several months. The berries contain a concentrated crimson juice that has been used as an ink, food coloring, and dye.

Young shoots: potherb; cooked vegetable; pickle. *Young leaves:* potherb. *Berries:* dye.

PURSLANE
Portulaca oleracea

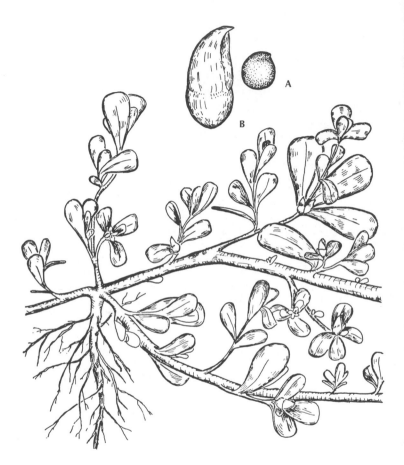

SIZE: Creeping plant, 1–2 in. high,
      covers about 1 sq. ft.

OTHER COMMON NAME: Pusley

HABITAT: In fertile sandy soil of old
         gardens, cultivated fields, and
         waste areas

SEASON: Summer to early fall, leaves
        and stems; late summer, seeds

IDENTIFYING CHARACTERISTICS: Purslane is a low, creeping plant that hugs the ground and spreads over large areas. It has many-branched stems that are smooth and succulent with reddish-green to purple coloration. The reddish-green leaves are very fat and fleshy and have a rounded triangular shape with the apex of the triangle at the base of the leaf. They are scattered on the stems, some being arranged alternately and others appearing to attach to the stem opposite each other. Leaves range from ½–2 in. in length. Small yellow flowers with 5 petals are borne at the forkings of the stems but bloom only in bright sunshine, usually in early morning, and wilt within a few hours. Numerous small black seeds (A) are crowded into seed pods (B) with a cap at the top that breaks open at maturity.

COLLECTION AND USE: Purslane has been used as a food plant for over 2000 years but is now quite unjustly regarded as an obnoxious weed. The juicy young *leaves* and *stems* are an excellent addition to salads and, because they contain so much water, are a thirst-quenching and slightly sour nibble in the field. Boiled, the top leaves and stems are a very good potherb that loses little bulk during cooking and has a slightly mucilaginous quality, rather like okra. Because of this quality, Purslane adds body to soups and stews. People who find this quality objectionable can mask it by combining cooked, chopped Purslane tops with beaten egg and bread crumbs and baking in a casserole. The thick stems at the base of the plant (often ¼ in. in diameter) can be pickled in vinegar and pickling spices. The numerous *seeds* can be collected by pulling entire plants from the ground and allowing them to dry. In drying, they will use their stored water to ripen all the seed pods, which otherwise would mature over an extended period of time. Then, spread the plants on a cloth and walk on them to free the seeds. Pick out the leaves and stems and use a sieve to separate the coarse trash. Remove the small trash by winnowing. Then grind into flour. The flour can be boiled into a mush or, better, used in baking. The flavor of Purslane flour is good and it can be used alone or mixed with wheat flour or cornmeal for making muffins, pancakes, etc.

Leaves: salad; potherb; trail nibble; thickener. *Stems*: pickle. *Seeds*: flour; cereal.

SPRING BEAUTY

Claytonia virginica
and *C. caroliniana*

SIZE: Up to 6 in. high
OTHER COMMON NAME: Fairy spuds
HABITAT: Rich woods, thickets, and
   mountain clearings; in the West,
   mountainous areas only
SEASON: Spring

IDENTIFYING CHARACTERISTICS: Spring Beauty is one of the first wood-land wildflowers to bloom in the spring. Its flowers are a pale pink to rose color with deeper colored veins in the petals. The flowers have 5 petals and contain 5 stamens. Flowers are borne in loose clusters at the top of smooth fragile stems that have a single pair of lance-shaped leaves lower down. The leaves are opposite and 1–6 in. long and ½–1½ in. wide. Anywhere from 1–40 flowering stems originate from a single enlarged underground stem, or corm. The corms are situated about 3 in. below ground level and range in size from ½–2 in. in diameter.

COLLECTION AND USE: Because of the small size of the *corms* and the deceptively large number of flowering stems put forth by each plant, it is difficult to collect an adequate supply of the edible corms unless the plant is growing in extreme abundance. However, if the plants are sufficiently abundant to warrant collecting, the result makes the effort well worthwhile. The corms should be washed thoroughly after being dug; they can then be either boiled or roasted like potatoes. They also make an excellent addition to stews. Spring Beauty corms need not be peeled before cooking, as the peels are not bitter; if removal is desired, it is most easily done after cooking. The taste of the corms is good, resembling potatoes but hinting at chestnuts. Their texture is smoother than either potatoes or chestnuts.

Corms: potato substitute.

CHICKWEED
Stellaria media

SIZE: Low reclining plant, stems up to
    12 in. long
HABITAT: In moist soil of waste areas,
    cultivated fields, and woods
SEASON: Spring through fall

IDENTIFYING CHARACTERISTICS: This plant has thread-like stems that are very weak and lie along the ground, forming loose mats at ground level. The stems branch frequently and have fine hairs arranged in rows along their lengths. The smooth-edged leaves are oval with rounded bases and sharply pointed tips. The lower leaves have leaf-stalks that are often covered with hairs; the upper leaves lack stalks and attach directly to the stems. The tiny flowers are white and star-shaped, having 5 deeply notched heart-shaped petals. The flowers bloom throughout the growing season. They occur singly in leafy clusters at the ends of the stems.

COLLECTION AND USE: The vigorous, rapidly growing *leaves* and *stems* of Chickweed can be eaten as a potherb from early spring until the plants are covered by winter snow. In fact, this hardy plant stays green under the snow and can be eaten during the winter if it can be found. Cooked greens of Chickweed have a taste that closely resembles spinach but are somewhat more bland. To preserve as much of the flavor as possible, overcooking should be avoided. The greens can also be used in salads and are best when mixed with more strongly flavored greens since they alleviate the bitterness of many spring greens and add a pleasant taste of their own. The leaves can be added to soups and stews as well. In all cases, only the tips of the stems should be used as the lower portions of the plant become stringy with maturity.

Leaves and *stems*: potherb; salad.

YELLOW POND LILY
Nuphar advena and related species

SIZE: Floating leaves 4–12 in. long

OTHER COMMON NAMES: Spatter dock,
   Cow lily, Water collard

HABITAT: Ponds, pools, and swamps;
   also tidal marshes

SEASON: Fall to early spring, roots; late
   summer and fall, seeds

IDENTIFYING CHARACTERISTICS: These are the familiar yellow-flowered water lilies of ponds and swamps. While there are numerous species with limited ranges, *N. advena* is by far the most common and widely distributed in the East; a similar species, *N. polysepalum,* predominates in the West. The leaves of *N. advena* are usually 4–12 in. long with broad rounded or elliptical blades that are deeply cleft at the base so that 2 rounded lobes extend back from the point of attachment of the thick, stout, and spongy leafstalks. The glossy leaves are usually raised several inches above the surface of the water. Immature leaves can be seen either floating or submerged. The long leafstalks extend to the bottom of the water where they rise directly from the top of a thick, fleshy rhizome (A). The flowers are borne singly on long stalks that also rise directly from the rootstock. The flower stalks stand erect above the surface of the water, usually holding the opened flowers above the level of the leaves. The flowers are nearly spherical cups made up of smooth, leathery petal-like sepals that enclose numerous small petals. The sepals and petals are golden-yellow (sometimes tinged with green or purple). When fully opened the flowers can reach 5 in. in diameter; they are followed by urn-shaped green to yellowish fruits (B) that are about 2 in. high and 2 in. across. The fruit is filled with seeds that are about the size and shape of popcorn kernels. (*N. advena* is illustrated.)

COLLECTION AND USE: This plant was an important source of food to the Indians: western tribes favored the seeds; eastern, the starchy rootstocks. When the seed pods ripen (late summer to early fall), they should be cut free of the stalk and allowed to dry in the sun. After drying they can be pulled apart; each releases a small handful of large *seeds*. The seeds provide a nutritious substitute for popcorn. While they do not burst as readily as kernels of popcorn, they do swell considerably during cooking and are tender with a good flavor. They can also be parched lightly over a slow fire or in an oven, pounded slightly and winnowed to remove the outer husk, and then either boiled and eaten like rice or ground into a meal and used like cornmeal as mush or in bread. The *roots* contain large quantities of starch from fall to early spring and in shallow water can easily be pulled free of the mud and used as a potato substitute. The roots can be boiled or roasted whole, or sliced and fried. Some people complain of a strong taste; this can be removed by boiling in 2 changes of water before eating or roasting or frying. Many, however, find the taste quite agreeable without this process.

Seeds: popcorn; flour; cereal. *Roots*: potato substitute.

MARSH MARIGOLD
Caltha palustris

SIZE: 6–12 in. high, but sometimes
    larger
OTHER COMMON NAMES: Cowslip,
    King-cup, May-blob
HABITAT: Swamps; wet meadows, fields,
    and woods—particularly in clay
    and limestone regions
SEASON: Spring to early summer; later in
    Northwest

IDENTIFYING CHARACTERISTICS: Marsh Marigold is a common spring wildflower having smooth bright yellow flowers that look a lot like buttercups but are much larger (up to 1½ in. in diameter). They have between 5 and 9 petal-like sepals and between 5 and 10 pistils. The plants have stout hollow stems that branch frequently and have small longitudinal furrows extending along their length. The rich green succulent leaves are rounded or kidney-shaped with wavy edges that have small rounded teeth. Size ranges from 3–6 in. across. Those at the base of the plant are on long, fleshy leafstalks; the leaves higher up are on much shorter stalks and the topmost leaves often have almost no leafstalk. Where the leafstalks join the stems of the plant there is a papery sheath that partly surrounds the stem. The leaves are arranged alternately on the stems.

COLLECTION AND USE: Up to and through its flowering season, the *young leaves* of this plant can be used as a potherb. Young leaves should be carefully selected and cut free from the plant; the papery sheaths on the leafstalks should be excluded. As a potherb, the plant has an acrid quality that can be removed by boiling in several changes of water. The *flower buds* can be used to make a substitute for capers by steeping them in boiling water and then pickling in either a salt solution or with vinegar and spices.

CAUTION: While there is little danger of confusing Marsh Marigold with the poisonous False Hellebore (*Veratrum viride,* see p. 210) or Water Hemlock (*Cicuta maculata,* see p. 215), both plants are common in the habitats occupied by Marsh Marigold. Consequently great care should be taken in gathering Marsh Marigold foliage to avoid including parts of either poisonous plant. Also, Marsh Marigold should never be eaten raw since it contains a toxic substance that is, however, completely destroyed by cooking.

Young leaves: potherb. *Flower buds*: pickle.

MAY APPLE
Podophyllum peltatum

SIZE: 1–2 ft. high
OTHER COMMON NAMES: American
    mandrake, Wild lemon
HABITAT: Rich moist soil of forests;
    sometimes pastures, woodland
    roadsides, and clearings
SEASON: Late summer

IDENTIFYING CHARACTERISTICS: May Apples rarely occur singly; usually, they carpet large sections of the forest floor with their big umbrella-like leaves. Plants are both fruit-bearing and nonfruit-bearing. The latter have a single leaf that is about 1 ft. in diameter that is attached at its center on the top of the single, unbranched stem. The leaf is round but deeply divided into 5–9 lobes. The outer edges of the lobes have a ragged, scalloped appearance and the area at the center of the leaf where the major veins of the lobes meet is shaped like a shield. In the fruiting plants (illustrated), the stem branches once and each branch bears a semicircular leaf with 3–7 lobes. The leaves are attached to the stems near their inner edges. The fruiting plants bear a single white flower, having a rather unpleasant smell, in the fork of the stem. The flower is 1½–2 in. in diameter and has either 6 or 9 waxy petals and twice that number of stamens. The fruit ripens in the late summer. When fully ripe it is a greenish-yellow color. The fruits (A) themselves are egg-shaped, about 2 in. long, and are borne in the fork of the stem. The skin of the fruit is relatively tough; inside, the seeds are arranged in lateral rows, each surrounded by a mass of sweet, gelatinous pulp.

COLLECTION AND USE: When May Apple *fruit* is fully ripe, the plants have already begun to die, the leaves are turning yellow, and the stems may have bent to the ground. At this stage the fruit falls into the hand when lightly touched. It may be eaten raw where it is found, providing a thirst-quenching snack in the field. Its flavor is sweet with a slight woodsy muskiness that makes some people love it and others dislike it. However, it loses all of its strangeness when cooked. It makes a delicious amber-colored jelly (remember to strain out the seeds after initial cooking) that is probably its best use. The fruit can also be stewed or the fragrant juice can be added to lemonade or other fruit juices or mixed with wine to make a punch.

CAUTION: Only the fruits of this plant are edible: the roots, seeds, and foliage contain a powerful cathartic. Although it was once used medicinally, it can be extremely toxic in uncontrolled doses.

Fruit: fresh; jelly; beverage.

BARBERRY

Berberis vulgaris and *B. canadensis*

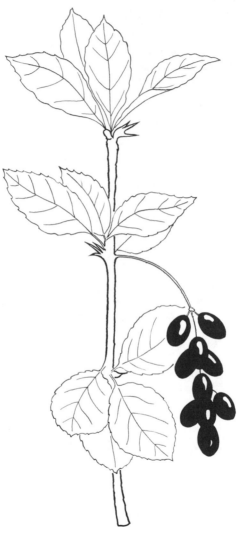

SIZE: Shrubs, 3–7 ft. tall
HABITAT: Rocky woods and escaped
    from cultivation along roads,
    fences, and in woods
SEASON: Fall and winter, fruit; spring,
    leaves

IDENTIFYING CHARACTERISTICS: There are a number of similar species of Barberry found throughout most of the U.S. One species, *B. vulgaris,* is a European plant that was widely cultivated as an ornamental hedge. Because it acts as a host for a stage in the life cycle of black wheat rust, it has been the subject of extermination campaigns in many parts of the country, although it can still be found. The most common native species is called *B. canadensis,* despite the fact that it is known as the American or Allegheny Barberry and is not found in Canada at all. Barberry is a spiny shrub that has yellow wood and yellow inner bark. The young, current year's shoots bear triple, or branched, spines and have few leaves; on the older branches, leaves attach just above the spines, either singly or in tight clusters. The leaves are about 1 in. long, are oval or spatula-shaped, and have toothed edges. The small (about ⅜ in. across), yellow, 6-petaled flowers hang from short flower stalks and are arranged alternately on a long drooping stem. The bright scarlet, 1-seeded berries likewise hang in long drooping clusters. *B. vulgaris* has branches that are gray in the second year and berries that are elliptical and about ¼ in. long; the branches of *B. canadensis* are brown with a purplish or reddish cast and the berries are slightly smaller and more rounded. Another species, *B. thunbergii,* the Japanese Barberry, bears sparse fruit that is too hard and dry to be of much use as food. It has single, unbranched spines and leaves with smooth edges.

COLLECTION AND USE: This common shrub, with its rather unappetizing spines, can provide a number of excellent food products. In the spring, the young *leaves* make a refreshing trail nibble. In the fall, the ripe *fruit* can be put to several uses. A tart, ruby-red jelly that is very good with meat can be made by simmering the fruit until the juice flows, pressing in a jelly bag, and boiling with an equal volume of sugar. No pectin is required. (If you boil the fruit in water, a larger quantity will result but commercial pectin will be needed for it to jell.) Barberry juice can also be added to jams and jellies of other fruits to add tartness and color. An acid, lemonade-like drink can be made by diluting the juice and adding sugar to taste. The berries can be cooked down with sugar to make a sauce that can be used like Cranberry sauce (see p. 167) but it is unpleasant to some people because of the presence of the many hard seeds. Barberries can be used to make pies and tarts as well but the same objection holds true. A pickle that makes a good relish can be made by mixing the fruit with an equal volume of sugar, covering with vinegar, boiling briefly, and storing in sealed jars. The yellow color of the *wood, inner bark, and roots* can be extracted by boiling in water (use small chips or sawdust) to make a yellow dye that was formerly much used.

Leaves: trail nibble. *Fruit:* jelly; beverage; sauce; pies; pickle. *Wood, bark, and roots:* yellow dye.

PAWPAW
Asimina triloba

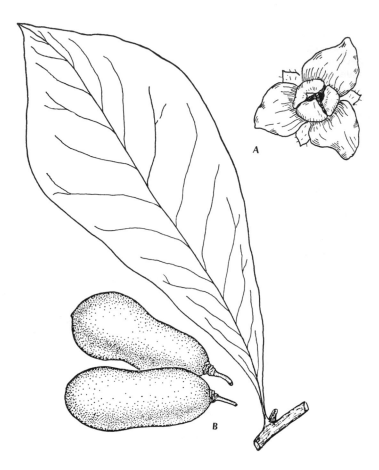

A

B

SIZE: Small tree, usually about 10 ft.
   high but can go up to 40 ft.
HABITAT: In shade of open woods,
   particularly along creeks and
   streams
SEASON: Fall

IDENTIFYING CHARACTERISTICS: The Pawpaw is the sole North American representative of this tropical family of plants. It is a small, shrub-like tree with a trunk that seldom exceeds 6 in. in diameter. The smooth, alternate leaves are 6–10 in. long at maturity with dark-green upper surfaces and lighter undersides. They are oval in shape but are broadest just below their abruptly pointed tips and taper gradually toward the base, where they join a short leafstalk. Young stems and opening leaves are covered with rust-colored down that falls off as they mature. The leaves and flowers open at the same time. The flowers (A) are attached to the branches at the sites occupied by the previous year's leaves. They are about 1–1½ in. in diameter and have 6 purple petals that are arranged in 2 layers. The outer 3 are large and spreading while the inner set is much smaller and stands up straight, forming a 3-pointed crown in the center of the flowers. The curved, cylindrical fruits (B) are 3–5 in. long and 1–1½ in. in diameter at maturity. They are green when unripe but gradually turn dark brown. Several flat seeds are surrounded by a mass of bright yellow pulp.

COLLECTION AND USE: Pawpaw *fruits* usually fall from the trees before they are fully ripe and can be collected from the ground. The fruit can also be pulled from the tree. In either case, they should be allowed to ripen before eating. When fully ripe, the pulp is sweet, with a creamy consistency that some people find objectionable, others delicious. Some people prefer to eat the fruit before it is fully ripe, at a stage where it has lost its acrid unripe taste but is still somewhat firm. In the northern part of its range, Pawpaw usually ripens after the first frosts of autumn. The fruit can be eaten fresh, baked, baked in pies, or pulped and mixed with eggs and gelatin and served chilled.

Fruit: fresh; pies; other desserts.

SASSAFRAS
Sassafras albidum

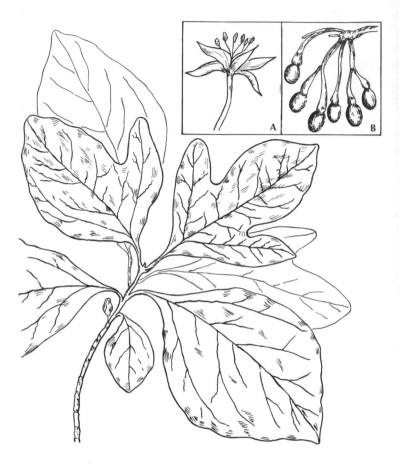

SIZE: Large shrub, up to 15 ft. high, particularly in northern part of range; in southern range, more commonly a small tree up to 50 ft. high

OTHER COMMON NAMES: Mitten plant, Cinnamonwood, Tea tree

HABITAT: Dry woods, thickets, and roadsides

SEASON: All year, roots; spring and summer, leaves

IDENTIFYING CHARACTERISTICS: The spicy, aromatic leaves and roots of this shrub or small tree have made it one of the better known plants in its range. The bark of larger specimens is reddish-brown, very thick, and rough; the young twigs and smaller branches have smooth green bark. The leaves vary greatly and 3 types can be found on the same plant, often on the same twig. The basic shape is oval but some leaves have a single lobe on one side that makes them resemble mittens with the lobe being the thumb. Others have 3 lobes with the largest in the center. The edges of the leaves are smooth. The leaves are arranged alternately on short (less than 1 in. long) leafstalks. Small greenish-yellow flowers (A) are borne in clusters and appear at the same time the leaves are unrolling in the spring. Later, oval blue berries (B) are borne on stout, club-shaped, reddish stalks.

COLLECTION AND USE: Sassafras was one of the first American plants to be exported to Europe where it was highly valued for medicinal properties. The *roots* and root bark are used to prepare a hot beverage that is drunk as tea. While Sassafras tea is primarily known as a stimulating medicinal tonic, it is also a pleasant beverage. Some people dislike it because they associate its flavor with medicine (the essential oil distilled from the roots has been widely used as a flavoring for medicines). To prepare tea, dig the roots, wash them thoroughly, and boil in water until it becomes a rich, red color. Since Sassafras grows in dense clumps and spreads by underground runners, it is easiest to use the roots of small plants that can be pulled from the ground; the thinning that results from gathering the roots will often be beneficial to the surrounding plants. Large quantities of root are not needed and a single piece of root can be boiled several times before all the flavor is gone. Root bark can be peeled free from the root, dried, and stored for use as tea. The dried root bark should be powdered, and about ½ teaspoon steeped in boiling water makes a cup of tea. Root bark that has been thoroughly dried gets very friable and can be eaten or used as spicing like cinnamon sticks. A pungent condiment for eating with meat used to be prepared by grating root bark into a boiling sugar solution. Because the *leaves* of Sassafras are extremely mucilaginous, they are used in the South to prepare "gumbo filet," or thickening. The leaves are dried, rubbed to a powder, and sifted free of stems and veins. The resulting fragrant powder can be used like flour or cornstarch to thicken soups, gravies, and stews. It is as effective as flour or cornstarch and imparts a subtle flavor.

CAUTION: The oil contained in Sassafras is said to be narcotic in action. No harmful effects have been reported when the plant is used in moderation but large doses should probably be avoided. Berries are not a food source.

Roots: tea; condiment. *Leaves*: thickener; flavoring.

MUSTARD
Brassica nigra
  and related species

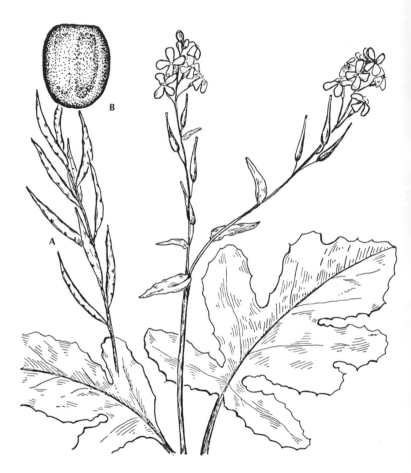

SIZE: Up to 6 ft. high at maturity;
    usually between 1 and 3 ft.
HABITAT: Waste areas and cultivated
    fields
SEASON: Spring, leaves; summer, seeds

IDENTIFYING CHARACTERISTICS: All members of the Mustard family are edible. The family is large and includes cultivated turnips, radishes, cresses, cabbage, and cauliflower. Erect, branching annuals, the Mustards of the *Brassica* genus grow as weeds throughout the U.S. and Canada. Black Mustard (*B. nigra*) is the variety most often used for food and is one of the most widespread. The stems of this plant are covered with scattered hairs, although occasionally they are nearly smooth. The lower leaves are on slender leafstalks and are large and lobed. They have a large terminal lobe followed by several pairs of smaller ones, all of which have fine teeth around the edges. The leaves further up the stems, those on the flower stalks in particular, are much smaller, have short or almost no leafstalks, lack lobes, and have edges that are not toothed. The leaves alternate on the stems. The flowers are typical of all plants in the Mustard family. They have 4 petals and 6 stamens—4 long ones and 2 short. The petals form the shape of a cross. The flowers of *B. nigra* are bright yellow, ¼–½ in. in diameter. They are borne in clusters along flower stalks that grow to about 2 ft. high. While the upper flowers are still opening, the lower ones are replaced by elongated, somewhat 4-sided seed pods (A) that stand erect along the flower stalk and are filled with small, dark brown seeds (B). (*B. nigra* is illustrated.)

COLLECTION AND USE: Black Mustard frequently grows in such profusion that entire fields are carpeted with its bright yellow flowers in the late spring. The young *leaves* can be used as a salad green or potherb but should be collected as early as possible since they rapidly become bitter as the plants mature. The lower leaves are generally less pungent than the upper ones and can be used until they exceed 4–6 in. in length. When used as a potherb, Mustard greens generally require 20–30 min. of boiling. They lose a great deal of bulk during cooking so a large quantity should be gathered. The *seeds* can be used to prepare table mustard or as a seasoning for meats and salads. The easiest way to collect Mustard seed is to gather the entire flower stalk when the lowest pods are ripe and just beginning to drop their seeds. Drying for several days on a flat surface or a plastic sheet will loosen the seeds in the immature pods. They can then be pounded free of the pods and the stems and pods winnowed out. The seeds can be either crushed or ground into a powder. Powdered Black Mustard seed is the same as the dried mustard sold in grocery stores. Table mustard can be prepared by mixing the powdered seed with flour, vinegar, and water. Powdered Mustard seed mixed with flour and water can be used as a mustard plaster for treating sore muscles.

Leaves: salad; potherb. *Seeds*: seasoning; condiment; medicine.

SHEPHERD'S PURSE
Capsella bursa-pastoris

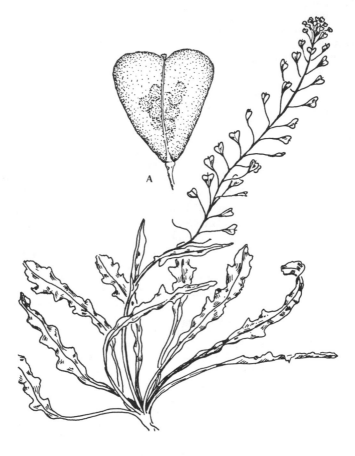

A

SIZE: 4–24 in. high

Other common names: Pickpocket,
    Shovelweed, Pepper-and-salt

HABITAT: Roadsides, gardens, lawns,
    and waste areas

SEASON: Spring and summer, leaves;
    fall, seeds

IDENTIFYING CHARACTERISTICS: Shepherd's Purse is a familiar garden weed. It has a rosette of leaves at ground level that are oblong and divided into irregular, opposite lobes; they look rather like Dandelion leaves. They range from 2–4 in. long. A single smooth stem rises from the center of the cluster of leaves; it sometimes branches toward the top. Small arrowhead-shaped leaves alternate on the stem. They lack leafstalks and their 2 lower lobes seem to wrap around the stem. The tiny white flowers have 4 petals that are arranged in 2 opposite pairs. The flowers are borne along elongated stalks that attach to the stems at the bases of the stem leaves; these flower-bearing stalks frequently account for half the height of the plant. Flowers alternate on the stalks and hang from slender stalks that are almost an inch long. The flowers are replaced by flat seed pods (A) that are triangular and are attached to short stalks at their apex. It is for these seed pods that this plant is named.

COLLECTION AND USE: This vigorous plant practically refuses to stop growing, even in winter, and consequently has a long season of usefulness as a food plant. It can usually be found in flower from very early spring until killing frosts, and in warm parts of its range it frequently flowers all winter. Young *leaves* have a peppery flavor; they make a good salad green and can be used as a potherb until the plant flowers. They are soft and require little cooking. Many describe the taste as a delicate cross between turnip greens and cabbage. Shepherd's Purse was once cultivated for its greens. The *seeds* were used by the California Indians as a source of meal. The seed pods should be collected, allowed to dry thoroughly, crushed to free the seed, winnowed, parched, and then ground into flour or cooked as mush. This is a great deal of work; a better use of the dried seed pods is as a seasoning. In soups and stews, they add a peppery quality.

Leaves: salad; potherb. *Seeds*: flour; cereal; seasoning.

WATER CRESS
Nasturtium officinale

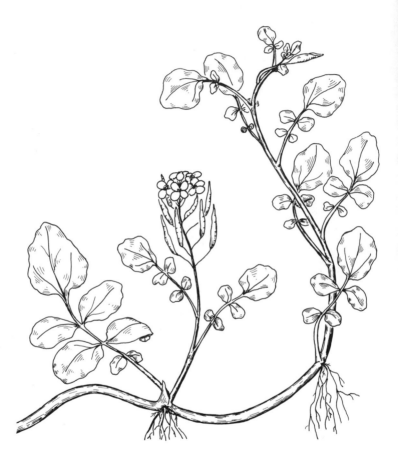

SIZE: Stems 6–18 in. long, floating or
    extending 2–4 in. above the water
HABITAT: In shallow, slowly moving
    water of cold brooks, ditches, and
    springs
SEASON: All year

IDENTIFYING CHARACTERISTICS: Water Cress is a cultivated plant that has gone wild with a vengeance. It can now be found across the U.S. and southern Canada although it is less common on the plains and is still rarely found in wilderness areas far from human habitation. Its jointed stems float in slow-moving water and send out roots from the joints that anchor it if it drifts into a suitable spot. These white roots are plainly visible hanging from floating stems. The leaves are pinnately compound and have from 3–11 smooth, rounded leaflets. The leaflets are smooth and fleshy, dark green, and have smooth edges but a slightly irregular outline. The terminal leaflet is always the largest and most irregularly shaped. The white flowers are borne in clusters at the ends of the stems and have 4 petals arranged in the shape of a cross. The flowers are replaced by elongated, somewhat flattened seed pods that are usually ½–1 in. long and contain 2 parallel rows of tiny seeds.

COLLECTION AND USE: The use of Water Cress as a food plant probably predates written records. Used by the ancient Persians, it was both recommended and derided by ancient Greek physicians, fed by the Romans to the insane, and among the earliest European plants introduced to North America. The lower parts of the stems get tough and stringy, so only the leafy leading ends of the *stems* need be collected. They can be snapped off without disturbing the plant. Its best use is as a raw salad green but it also makes an excellent potherb that requires only the barest amount of cooking. It is a good addition to soups and stews.

CAUTION: When Water Cress is to be eaten raw, it should be disinfected unless the water in which it is growing is of unquestionable purity. Harmful bacteria of polluted water can cling to the stems and are not removed by normal rinsing. The easiest way is to wash in water containing a water purification tablet of the type sold in most camping supply stores (see p. 3). If the leaves are then rinsed in plain water, no chemical flavor will remain.

Leaves and stems: salad; potherb.

HORSERADISH
Amoracia Lapathifolia

SIZE: Up to 3 ft. tall
OTHER COMMON NAME: Sting nose
HABITAT: Moist soil
SEASON: Spring, young leaves; all year,
    root

IDENTIFYING CHARACTERISTICS: The Horseradish is a plant that was introduced into North America by early English settlers but has spread from cultivation. It is a perennial that spreads very slowly but once established will continue to flourish almost indefinitely. Its presence in the wilderness is often an indication of a former homesite even though all visible traces may be long gone. Horseradish is a large plant with large oblong leaves up to 15 in. long and 6–8 in. wide. The leaves have long leafstalks with a channel down their middles and thick, stiff midribs in the leaf blades. They have wavy edges and rise directly from a long, white, vertical root that may be 2 in. in diameter and up to 1 foot long. Toward the tip the root forms branches. In the early summer, the plants send up a single erect flower stalk that sometimes reaches a height of 3–4 ft. Small, lance-shaped leaves without leafstalks alternate along its length. The tip of the flower stalk eventually forms several branches that have small, white, 4-petaled flowers clustered at their upper ends. These plants rarely form seeds, propagating mainly by extension of their root system, but if they do, the seed pods are egg-shaped and have a vertical line running around them, dividing them into halves.

COLLECTION AND USE: Horseradish is best known for the pungent condiment that is prepared by grating the root. The best way to tell if you have the right plant is to scrape a few fragments from a freshly dug root and place them on the tip of your tongue. The hot, pungent taste should be immediately evident. No pungent smell or taste is evident from an unbruised or uncut root; the active material is produced by a chemical reaction that begins when the root is crushed. For this reason, the more pungent the horseradish desired, the finer it should be grated. In the early spring, the *young leaves* can be eaten as a potherb like Mustard greens (see p. 105) but they are even more peppery so they are best when mixed with blander potherbs. Small quantities added to salads also add a peppery quality. Both the leaves and the *roots* have figured in herbal remedies mainly as a diuretic, stimulant, and antiseptic for the digestive tract.

Young leaves: potherb; salad; medicine. *Roots:* condiment; seasoning; medicine.

WINTER CRESS
Barbarea vulgaris and *B. verna*

SIZE: 1–2 ft. high at maturity

OTHER COMMON NAMES: Yellow rocket,
  Spring cress, Upland cress, Belle
  Isle cress (*B. verna*)

HABITAT: *B. vulgaris* in rich soil of
  streambanks and low areas; *B.
  verna* in meadows and fields

SEASON: Late fall, winter, early spring

IDENTIFYING CHARACTERISTICS: Both species of Winter Cress are hardy plants characterized by a rosette of smooth leaves that remains bright green through the winter and sends up lush new growth during winter warm spells. The generic name, *Barbarea,* comes from the fact that Winter Cress can be gathered for fresh greens on December 4, St. Barbara's Day. The glossy and hairless leaves rise directly from the rootstock of the plant. They have a large terminal lobe followed by a series of smaller lateral lobes farther down. In *B. verna* there are 5–10 pairs of lateral lobes; *B. vulgaris* has between 1 and 4 pairs. The leafstalks are stout and angular and broaden at the base to clasp the bases of other leaves. In the early spring, Winter Cress puts up a stout stem that will grow to between 1 and 2 ft. high and in early summer this bears small yellow flowers in clusters at its summit. The flowers are typical of the Mustard family, having 4 petals arranged in a cross shape and 6 stamens, 4 long and 2 short. Later, the flowers are replaced by elongated 4-sided seed pods that stand upright along the stem. (*B. vulgaris* is illustrated.)

COLLECTION AND USE: The *leaves* of Winter Cress can be used as a salad green or a potherb from the time the weather turns cold and frosty in the fall until after the last frost in the spring. From the time flower stems appear in the spring until the first killing frosts of the fall, the leaves are generally too bitter to be eaten. Even during the cold seasons of the year, the greens of Winter Cress are somewhat bitter, but no more so than such common cultivated greens as endive. In fact, one species, *B. verna,* is cultivated in Europe and the southern U.S., the crop being grown when fields would otherwise lie fallow. For some people, the greens may be too bitter to serve as the major ingredient of a salad, but they are generally acceptable when mixed with blander greens. As a potherb, much of the bitterness can be removed by boiling in a second change of water. The greens lose considerable bulk during cooking so an ample supply should be gathered.

Leaves: salad; potherb.

GOOSEBERRY AND CURRANT
Ribes; many species

SIZE: Shrubs, 2–5 ft. high
HABITAT: Woods, usually moist but
sometimes dry; some species
prefer rocky places, others
swamps
SEASON: Summer

IDENTIFYING CHARACTERISTICS: The plants in this genus are all rather small shrubs that bear edible berries. The leaves are palmately lobed and veined with edges that have coarse teeth. The exact shape of the leaves varies greatly from species to species; some have 5 clearly defined lobes; others are less obviously lobed and appear to have fewer lobes. The leaves are arranged alternately on young branches; they occur in clusters on short lateral branches that are in their first year of growth. The flowers are borne on drooping stalks that rise from the stems at the bases of the leafstalks. In some species, several flowers are attached alternately to a single stalk; in others, flowers occur in clusters with a single flower to a stalk; occasionally there is but a single flower. The flowers (A) have 5 petals and 5 sepals and are small; coloration varies from greenish- or yellowish-white to purple. The fruits (B) are many-seeded berries about ¼–⅓ in. in diameter with crown-like appendages at their bases; close examination shows these appendages are composed of 5 shriveled segments. Fruit ranges from black to purple, red, or yellow. The *Ribes* plants are loosely divided into 2 groups: Gooseberry and Currant. Gooseberry generally has thorny stems with thorns particularly evident at the point where leaves attach to the stems. The fruit is frequently covered with fine spines (although some species bear smooth-skinned fruit) and is firmly joined to the stalks. Currant is less likely to have thorny stems: its fruits are smooth-skinned and separate easily from the stalks. (Red currant [*R. triste*] is illustrated.)

COLLECTION AND USE: While all members of this large group of plants (there are more than 80 species in North America) bear edible *fruit,* the quality varies widely. In many species, the fruit is sweet enough to be eaten fresh but a number of others have sour fruit and these are best when cooked with the addition of sugar. Because of the spines on Gooseberries, most people prefer them cooked, but they can be eaten raw if chewed thoroughly. Both Gooseberries and Currants can be used in pies, and jams and jellies of excellent quality can be made from them. The fruit of Currants makes a good wine. The fruit can be preserved by drying or used in making pemmican, an Indian trail food (see p. 14).

Fruit: fresh; jams and jellies; wine; pemmican.

MOUNTAIN ASH
Pyrus, species of subgenus *Sorbus*

SIZE: Large shrubs or small trees up to
    30 ft. high

OTHER COMMON NAMES: Roundwood,
    Dogberry, Rowan tree

HABITAT: Woods, roadsides, rocky
    slopes

SEASON: Fall (after frosts) and winter

IDENTIFYING CHARACTERISTICS: These are small trees with smooth bark and alternate, pinnately compound leaves generally having either 13 or 15 leaflets. The leaflets have yellow-green upper surfaces and are lance-shaped or oval with sharp serrations around their edges. The flowers are white with 5 petals and are borne in rather flat-topped, dense clusters. The flowers are replaced by red-orange fruits that begin to ripen in late summer or early fall. The fruits form dense clusters that cover the trees and are particularly visible after the leaves have fallen. They are about ¼ in. in diameter and are on short stems like cherries.

COLLECTION AND USE: Mountain Ash belongs to a small group of plants that hold their *fruits* through the winter with the result that they can be gathered in the wild during the cold months of the year. They should be collected only after they have been frozen. Before freezing they are only partially ripe and very sour with a rather unpleasant taste. Repeated freezing improves the quality of the fruit until it can be quite good. The fruit of Mountain Ash can be eaten raw but it usually has a fairly mealy texture. It is better stewed and sweetened with sugar and provides a welcome addition to the diet of the person in the wilderness in winter. It can also be used in pies, and in jellies and jams (without commercial pectin). Mountain ash berries, like almost everything else containing even a hint of sugar, have also been used to make wine.

Fruit: fresh; pies; jam; wine.

JUNEBERRY
Amelanchier; numerous species

SIZE: Large bush (5 ft. high) or small
tree (up to 30 ft. high)
OTHER COMMON NAMES: Shadbush,
Serviceberry, Sugarplum
HABITAT: Clearings and borders of
woods, especially in burns or new
clearings; some species in rocky
areas, others in swamps
SEASON: Summer to fall, when ripe
(varies by range)

IDENTIFYING CHARACTERISTICS: The *Amelanchier* genus is represented in North America by 19 species, all bearing palatable fruit. Most species grow in dense clumps although solitary plants are also found. Juneberry bushes have smooth branches with gray bark. Leaves vary from species to species but are generally elliptical to oblong with blunt, rounded bases and pointed tips. They have short slender leaf-stalks, are arranged alternately on the branches, and have edges that range from coarsely toothed to finely serrated or almost smooth. When plants are in flower in the early spring they are very conspicuous and can be marked for summer berrying. Juneberry flowers have 5 petals, are about 1 in. in diameter, and are white, or sometimes pink. They appear before the leaves are fully opened and are borne in profusion in loose, hanging clusters. The fruit is red, becoming purple-black when fully ripe; it hangs from slender stalks in clusters. Individual berries are round or pear-shaped and about ¼ in. in diameter. The end of each berry has 5 tooth-like projections similar to those on a blueberry. Juneberries have 10 large, soft seeds.

COLLECTION AND USE: Early explorers of North America were quick to mark the Juneberry as one of the best native fruits but in modern times it has been strangely neglected. The *berries* are sweet and juicy, of excellent flavor, and can be found virtually anywhere in the U.S. and Canada. There is a certain amount of local variation in the quality of the fruit—some plants fruiting heavily with sweet, juicy berries and others having berries of inferior quality. The easiest way to use the berries is simply to eat them off the bush but they also make excellent pies and sauces. The cooked berries can be added to muffins and pancakes. Juneberries were preserved by American Indians for winter use by drying crushed berries and then compressing them into cakes. Dried berries can be stewed or cooked with meat. The Indians also used them in pemmican, a nearly ideal trail food. Dried berries were mixed with dried meat that had been pounded to a fine paste, animal fat was kneaded in, and the mass was formed into cakes. Juneberries mixed with commercially available dried beef and suet make a good imitation of the Indian product (see p. 14).

Berries: fresh; pies; pemmican.

HAWTHORN
Crataegus; many similar species

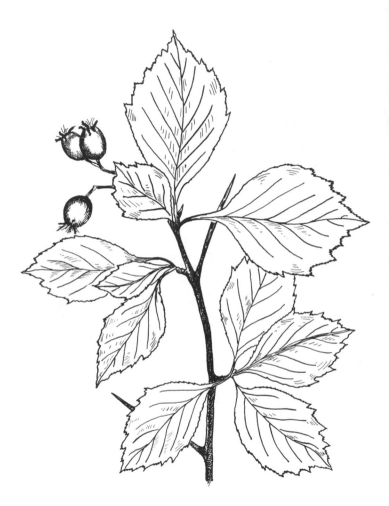

SIZE: Shrubs to small trees up to 25 ft.
    high

OTHER COMMON NAMES: Haw, Red
    haw, Thorn

HABITAT: Extremely varied—in wet and
    dry, rocky, or rich woods and
    fields

SEASON: Fall

IDENTIFYING CHARACTERISTICS: Despite the confusion the numerous species of this genus have created in the botanical world, Hawthorns are readily recognized by the amateur. What clearly distinguishes them from other North American trees and shrubs is the presence of fierce thorns from 1–5 in. long on the smaller branches and often on the larger ones as well. The branches are crooked and irregular. Hawthorns have leaves that may be simple in outline or lobed in various ways but they always have serrations on their edges. In the spring they are covered with clusters of 5-petaled flowers that are usually white, but are red or pink in a few species. The flowers look very much like those of apple trees, to which they are closely related. The fruits are red when fully ripe, although a few species have fruits that are yellow, blue, or black. They look like tiny apples and contain from 1–5 hard nutlets.

COLLECTION AND USE: Hawthorn *fruits* vary greatly from species to species and even from tree to tree in the amount of pulp and quality of flavor. When eaten raw they are rarely good but experimentation will show that some are vastly better than others. In a pinch, though, the fresh fruits are worth knowing because they are quite nutritious. They may also be dried or mixed into pemmican (see p. 14). By far the best use of these astringent fruits is in making jams and jellies. Unlike the fresh fruit, jams and jellies made from Hawthorn are of excellent quality. The fruit contains enough natural pectin to jell without the addition of the commercial variety. The *thorns* are very strong and extremely sharp. They are useful as awls for punching holes and for improvised fishhooks.

Fruit: jams and jellies. *Thorns:* awls; fishhooks.

STRAWBERRY
Fragaria vesca, F. virginiana, and related species

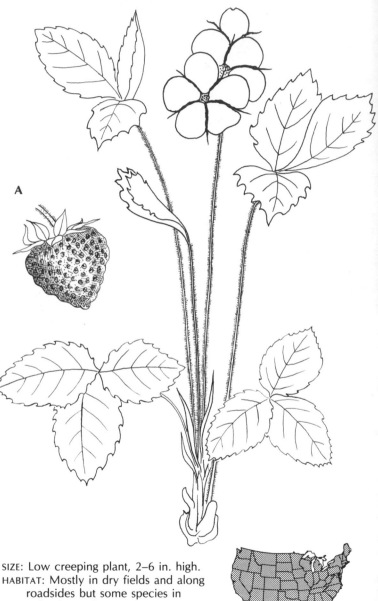

A

SIZE: Low creeping plant, 2–6 in. high.
HABITAT: Mostly in dry fields and along
    roadsides but some species in
    upland woods
SEASON: Early summer

IDENTIFYING CHARACTERISTICS: There is almost no mistaking a Strawberry plant when it is loaded with ripe, red fruit. Clusters of 2–9
strawberries hang off the top of a long, usually hairy, stem that rises
directly from the ground. They are usually bright red (although there
is a white form that occurs rarely) and the outside of the berry is
covered by tiny seed-like fruits (A) that are either situated in pits (in
F. virginiana) or on the surface (in *F. vesca*). Each berry has a "hull"
of 10 tiny, green, leaf-like parts that cup the top. However, Strawberry
plants are every bit as conspicuous in the spring when their tiny, white,
5-petaled flowers appear in clusters at the top of the stem that later
holds the berries. The dark green leaves are on slender leafstalks that
rise directly from ground level where they attach to a horizontal
rhizome. They are palmately compound and have 3 oval or pointed
leaflets that attach directly to the leafstalk. The leaflets have toothed
edges. Strawberry plants spread freely by sending out runners, or
stolons, at ground level and are rarely found singly. They usually form
large colonies.

COLLECTION AND USE: Since Strawberries frequently grow in grassy
fields and have very small berries, they are easier to spot in the spring
when surrounding plants have not grown high enough to hide them
and their delicate white flowers. The uses of the *fruit* need little
explanation. Although they are much smaller than cultivated strawberries, their sweetness and flavor are so superior that the extra care
required to pick them is well worth the effort. Because strawberries
are so delicate and easily squashed, remove the "hulls" before they
are placed in a container; picking over them later is almost impossible.
They can be used just like cultivated strawberries in jams and jellies,
pies, and sauces, as well as eaten fresh, either at home or in the field.
You can also make the berries into a refreshing cold beverage by
crushing them and adding water and sugar to taste. Wild strawberries
can be preserved by drying. Mash ripe berries into a pulp and spread
it thinly on flat surfaces such as cookie sheets. Place the pulp in the
sun (covered with kitchen film or cheesecloth to keep off insects) or
in a slow oven until it has dried to a leathery consistency and can be
peeled free of the pan. In the sun this will take several days—be sure
to take it inside at night. A dusting of powdered sugar will keep it from
becoming sticky, and it can be stored in sealed jars. It can either be
eaten as a confection or soaked in water and used as a substitute for
fresh fruit in sauces, pies, etc. Herbalists have long attributed medicinal properties to Strawberries, and their intuition is borne out by the
finding that they contain exceptionally high levels of vitamin C, both
in the leaves and the fruit. When fruit is not present, steeping the
leaves in boiling water will make a vitamin C rich tea that can be used
as a breakfast beverage in the field or at home. The leaves can also
be preserved for winter use by drying, and storing in sealed jars.

Fruit: fresh; jams and jellies; pies; cold beverages; confections.
Leaves: tea.

ROSE
Rosa; many species

SIZE: Shrubs, 2–8 ft. tall

HABITAT: Species found in dry fields, open woods, roadsides, swamps and marshes, and around old homesites

SEASON: Summer, flowers; fall and winter, fruits; spring and summer, leaves

IDENTIFYING CHARACTERISTICS: There are more than 100 species of Rose growing wild in the U.S., and since they readily hybridize with one another, even botanists have trouble keeping them straight. But this is of little concern to the wild-food hunter. The Roses found in the wild vary in size from climbing varieties with long trailing canes to shrubs ranging from 2 to 8 ft. in height. In all but a few rare species the canes are equipped with thorns. The leaves are pinnately compound and are composed of between 3 and 11 leaflets, depending on the species. The leaflets are oval and have pointed tips in some species and rounded in others; the edges of the leaflets are toothed. Rose flowers are very fragrant and range from red to yellow to white. They have 5 delicate spreading petals that are usually between ½ and 1½ in. long and are almost as wide at their outer edge as they are long. They are borne singly or in loose clusters. The petals are attached to the edge of an urn-shaped receptacle that is a swelling of the end of the stem that supports the flower. At the narrowed top end of the receptacle are 5 leaf-like sepals, 1 for each petal. After the petals fall, the receptacle becomes more fleshy and swells as hard bony seeds form inside it. As these fruit mature, the receptacles begin to take on color, usually changing from green to orange to red as fall approaches. These swollen, colored receptacles sometimes reach 1 in. in length and are commonly known as rose hips (A).

COLLECTION AND USE: In the summer, the petals of Rose *flowers* can be nibbled while on the trail, added to salads, pancakes, muffins, and eggs as a fragrant seasoning, or made into a colorful jelly by mashing a couple of cups of petals into sugar and boiling rapidly with commercial pectin or by adding mashed petals to apple jelly. With a relatively simple distillation apparatus, the essence of the Rose flower can be distilled off into water. The resulting Rose water is widely used as a seasoning and flavoring. As a food source, though, the *fruit,* or rose hips, are far and away the more important. Rose hips' vitamin C content is about 60 times that of lemons and about 24 times that of oranges. Rose hips can be collected from the time they ripen in the late summer and fall, through the winter, and well into the following spring. The size of the rose hips varies and it is to the collector's advantage to look around for plants with the largest hips. Cut the hip free from the stem and snip off the 5 shriveled sepals. Rose hips can be eaten as stewed fruit; boiled down and strained to remove the seeds and used to make either jelly or "fruit soup"; or slit and the seeds removed, and boiled with water, sugar, and commercial pectin to make jam. Rose hips can also be dried, then ground into an easily stored meal that can be reconstituted by adding water and boiling. The *leaves* (dried) or the *petals* (fresh) can be steeped in water for a tea.

Flowers: trail nibble; seasoning; jelly; tea. *Fruit:* jams and jellies. *Leaves:* tea.

PURPLE AVENS
Geum rivale

SIZE: 1–2 ft. high
OTHER COMMON NAMES: Water avens,
    Chocolate root
HABITAT: Wet meadows and fields;
    swamps and bogs
SEASON: All year

IDENTIFYING CHARACTERISTICS: The stiff, slender stems of this plant are tinted with purple and are sometimes slightly hairy. The leaves are very irregular. A few pinnately compound leaves often reaching 12 in. in length rise directly from the rootstock. These leaves usually have 3 principal leaflets, but occasionally have 5. The terminal leaflet is the largest and is divided into 3 lobes of varied distinctness. The lower pair of principal leaflets is smaller. The leaflets are usually shaped like triangles that attach to the stem at one of their points and have coarse teeth around their edges. Below the principal leaflets there are from a few to many much smaller leaflets that vary widely in shape. The leaves along the stems are very small and get smaller and less frequent toward the top of the stem. They also vary greatly in shape, being toothed, lobed, and divided in a number of ways. Several flowers on long drooping stalks are borne at the top of the stem. They are bell-shaped with the bell being made up of 5 purple segments holding 5 petals that are yellow with vivid purple veins. The fruit is a bristly ball that is about ¾ in. in diameter. Each spiny bristle holds a seed that is spread by sticking to passing animals and humans.

COLLECTION AND USE: The horizontal *roots* of Purple Avens contain a substance that has a flavor resembling chocolate. A beverage that can be used as a substitute for hot chocolate is prepared by boiling the root in water. This imparts a chocolate-like flavor, but the root is not sweet and has a slightly astringent and acid quality. This can be masked by the addition of liberal amounts of sugar. Adding powdered milk to the Avens-flavored water also improves the beverage. In 16th-century England, the roots were soaked in wine, imparting a delicate fragrance. Wine flavored with Avens root was reputed to be a heart tonic.

Roots: chocolate flavoring; beverage.

BLACKBERRY, DEWBERRY, RASPBERRY
Rubus; many species

SIZE: Erect, bent, or trailing canes up to
   7 ft. long
OTHER COMMON NAMES: Wineberry,
   Cloudberry, Thimbleberry,
   Plumboy
HABITAT: Dry or moist woods, fields,
   and roadsides
SEASON: Spring, shoots; summer, fruits
   and leaves

IDENTIFYING CHARACTERISTICS: The members of the *Rubus* genus, known collectively as Brambles, are numerous and differ from each other slightly but all have edible fruit and are so distinctive as a group that mistaken identification is rare. The plants send up thorny stems or canes from ground level that form patches so dense they are often virtually impossible to walk through; some species have drooping canes and reproduce themselves by taking root when the tip of the cane bends down and touches the ground. Although the plants are perennials, the canes themselves are biennial. In their first year they are unbranched and do not produce flowers or fruit; the second year they do not increase in length but send out short branches that end in a flower cluster. The leaves on first-year canes of most species are compound and usually have 3 or 5 leaflets arranged palmately, although some species have 7 leaflets and are pinnately compound. The branched second-year canes have fewer, smaller leaves that are often not compound. The leaflets are usually pointed and have toothed edges. The flowers have 5 petals and are usually white, although some species have greenish-white or reddish flowers. The flowers vary from ¼ to ½ in. across and are borne in clusters at the ends of the second-year canes. The berries are composed of numerous juicy spheres, each containing a single seed arranged around a white central core. Where the stems attach, the fruit is cupped by 5 green, leaf-like appendages. The fruit is divided into two main groups: the first includes the Blackberries and Dewberries, and the second, the Raspberries. The fruit of the Blackberries and Dewberries is black or bluish-black and when picked breaks free of the plant with its stem and core intact. Blackberries have upright canes and Dewberries have canes that trail along the ground. The Raspberries have fruit that is either red or black, but when they are picked the fruit pulls free, leaving the core on the plant.

COLLECTION AND USE: Blackberries and raspberries may be used to make jellies, jams, sauces, and pies, or eaten fresh, plain or with cream. The juice, squeezed from fresh berries or extracted by boiling, is good mixed into sour fruit drinks like lemonade or those made from Sumac (see p. 141) or Barberry (see p. 99). Blackberry brandy or blackberry-flavored cordials can be made by adding blackberry juice to brandy or other alcohols and sweetening with sugar syrup. Fermented, they make a pleasant, sweet fruit wine. A tonic-like blackberry beverage can be made by packing berries in jars, covering with vinegar, letting stand sealed in a dark place for about 1 month, and decanting into clean bottles. It is served by mixing with water and ice, and sweetening with sugar. The *leaves* can be used in the field as a substitute for tea or dried in the sun or a slow oven for later use. Peeled, the new *shoots* in the spring make a trail nibble.

Fruit: fresh; jelly; pies; beverage; wine. *Leaves:* tea. *Shoots:* trail nibble.

BLACK CHERRY AND CHOKE CHERRY
Prunus serotina and *P. virginiana*

SIZE: *P. serotina* reaches 100 ft. but begins fruiting at about 15 ft.; *P. virginiana* seldom exceeds 20 ft.

HABITAT: *P. serotina* in forests but also along roadsides and fences; *P. virginiana* in borders of woods, roadsides, and swamps, and in thickets

SEASON: Late summer and early fall

IDENTIFYING CHARACTERISTICS: Wild Cherries bear only a superficial resemblance to the cultivated varieties; even when the latter have "run wild" they are still easily identified. The Black Cherry *(P. serotina)* is a large forest tree with dark bark on the mature trunk and reddish bark on the branches. The inner bark is aromatic. Its leaves are thick and shiny, oblong to lance-shaped with blunt teeth along their edges. They range from 1½–6 in. long and have a prominent midrib that is plainly visible on the underside. The flowers in the spring are white. The fruit is dark red but turns purplish-black as it ripens. The fruits are between ¼ and ⅓ in. in diameter and are borne in long clusters at the ends of the current year's twigs. The clusters are 3–6 in. long and resemble bunches of grapes. Choke Cherry *(P. virginiana)* is similar except that it lacks aromatic inner bark, and its leaves are thinner, more oval in shape, abruptly pointed, and have sharp fine teeth along their edges. The fruit is dark red or crimson and is borne in shorter clusters than that of Black Cherry. (*P. serotina* is illustrated.)

COLLECTION AND USE: Black Cherry is sometimes known as Rum Cherry because its *fruits* were widely used by early colonists to flavor rum and other liquors. They have a rich winey flavor and, despite a hint of bitterness, can be eaten raw. The fruit is collected from young trees with branches that can be reached from the ground or readily climbed; mature trees frequently have 50 ft. of unbranched trunk (hence their use as a valuable source of fine cabinet wood). Choke Cherry's name is well deserved: the fruit is too bitter and astringent to be eaten fresh, but cooking removes its astringency. Both Choke Cherries and Black Cherries make excellent jellies, each with an individual character. They lack pectin though, so commercial pectin or the juice of apples should be used to promote jelling. Pies can be made from Black Cherries but pitting the small fruits is tedious. The fruit of either can be added to muffins or pancakes. The easiest way is to prepare a sauce by boiling with sugar before adding them to the batter. The same sauce, chilled and with water added, makes a good cold fruit soup or beverage. The fruits can also be used to make wine.

CAUTION: The pits of wild cherries (like those of cultivated varieties and of plums, apricots, and peaches) contain toxic levels of hydrocyanic acid, or cyanide. It is destroyed by cooking, but raw pits should be avoided.

Fruit: fresh; pies; beverage; soup; jelly; wine.

WILD PLUM
Prunus; several species

A

SIZE: Large shrubs or small trees, 5–20 ft. tall

HABITAT: Moist woods, thickets, streambanks, and bottomlands; *P. maritima* in dunes and sandy coastal soil

SEASON: Summer

IDENTIFYING CHARACTERISTICS: Plums are close relatives of the Cherries, so close in fact that they are included in the same genus, *Prunus.* They are most easily distinguished from the Cherries (see p. 130) by differences in their fruit. While Cherries have more or less round, shiny fruit with a single round pit, plums are a little less round and have a groove or indentation that runs around the fruit from top to bottom and seems to split it into two halves (A). They have flattened pits rather than round ones and the fruit is covered with a whitish "bloom" that is lacking in the Cherries. In general, the Plums are large shrubs or small trees that seldom grow taller than 20 ft. They usually have rough bark and sometimes have blunt, rough thorns on their branches. The leaves are simple, range from lance-shaped to oval with serrated edges, have rather short leafstalks, and alternate on the branches. The delicate flowers, which appear before the leaves, are usually white and look very much like Cherry blossoms with 5 spreading petals surrounding numerous (15–20) stamens. One of the best-known Wild Plums in the East is the Beach Plum, *P. maritima.* It grows in sand dunes and sandy coastal soil along the eastern seaboard and bears purple or bluish-purple fruit. *P. americana,* the Wild Plum, is found throughout most of the U.S. and produces fruit that is red or yellow. The Canada Plum, *P. nigra,* grows across southern Canada and extends well down into the U.S. reaching south to Georgia and west to Iowa. It has light red or reddish-orange fruit. The Wild Goose Plums, *P. hortulana* and *P. Munsoniana,* have red and sometimes yellow fruit and are found in the Mississippi valley. *P. angustifolia,* the Chickasaw Plum, has red fruit and grows from New Jersey south to Florida and west to Texas. The Pacific or California Plum, *P. subcordata,* has dark red fruit and is found in southern Oregon and northern California. All Wild Plums bear fruit that varies from tree to tree and place to place. As a general rule, the fruit of Wild Plums is small, ranging from ½ to 1½ in. in diameter. (*P. americana* is illustrated.)

COLLECTION AND USE: Because of the small size of the *fruit,* the large size of the pits, and the variability of the quality of the fruit, it is best not to plan on stuffing with sweet fruit if you find a group of ripe Wild Plums; this is one fruit that has been improved almost beyond recognition by cultivation and breeding. However, trees with sweet fruit can be found, and if you're lucky enough to find one, by all means eat your fill. The best use of wild plums is still in jams, jellies, and conserves and they are well worth seeking for that use alone. In the field they can be quite good as stewed fruit. Plums also can be used to make a sweet fruit wine and have been used to flavor liquor in the same manner as the Black Cherry (see p. 131). Steeping in alcohol or vodka makes a liquor reminiscent of sloe gin.

CAUTION: Like the cherries, the pits of wild plums contain high levels of toxic hydrocyanic acid, or cyanide. It is destroyed by heat, but the tempting nut-like core of the pits should not be eaten raw.

Fruit: fresh; jams and jellies; wine.

GROUNDNUT
Apios americana

A

SIZE: Twining vine, stems up to 5 ft. long

OTHER COMMON NAMES: Bog potato, Indian potato, Hopniss, Wild bean

HABITAT: Rich thickets along streams or on low ground

SEASON: All year, tubers; summer, seed pods

IDENTIFYING CHARACTERISTICS: This is a slender vine that twines around bushes, ferns, and other nearby plants. The stems are smooth and soft with a milky juice. It has pinnately compound leaves with 3–9 oblong- to lance-shaped leaflets that are pointed at the ends and rounded at the bases. The leaflets have smooth edges and very short stalks. They are arranged opposite one another on the stalks. Groundnut flowers in late summer. The flowers look like those of the cultivated "sweet pea." They are purplish-brown, about ½ in. across, and are borne in dense clusters at the bases of the leaves. They are very fragrant, having a smell much like violets. After flowering, seed pods (A) resembling those of peas or beans (both are members of this family) are formed. They are fairly straight, slender, and grow to about 3 in. long. The root is shallow and rope-like with a series of tuberous swellings distributed along its length like beads on a string. They range from 1–3 in. in diameter. Dried Groundnut vines become very white and are fairly easy to spot in winter.

COLLECTION AND USE: Groundnut *tubers* were a staple source of food for the eastern American Indians and were widely used by early colonists. The tubers have a smooth texture and a rather sweet, pleasant taste. They can be cooked in any of the ways generally used for potatoes although they are better when boiled in salted water or sautéed in butter or bacon fat than when roasted. They can be eaten raw but the juice leaves an unpleasant, viscous film in the mouth; once cooked, this quality disappears. The ripe *seed pods* can be eaten as a substitute for beans; they should be boiled in salted water. They are, however, rarely found in sufficient quantity to provide much of a meal.

Tubers: potato substitute. *Seed pods:* cooked vegetable.

HOG PEANUT
Amphicarpa bracteata

A

SIZE: Twining vine, stems up to 3 ft. long

HABITAT: Rich woodlands, cool damp thickets, and stream banks

SEASON: Late fall to early spring

IDENTIFYING CHARACTERISTICS: Hog Peanut is a bean-like perennial vine with stems that climb surrounding vegetation by twining. The delicate stems, which grow up to 3 ft. long, are usually unbranched; when they do branch it is near the base of the plant. It has alternate, pinnately compound leaves with 3 equal-sized leaflets in a triangular arrangement. The leaflets are basically oval in shape with pointed tips and rounded bases. They range from 1–2 in. in length. The stems are covered with long brown hairs and the leaves frequently have a sparse covering of hairs on both sides. What best characterizes this plant is that it produces 2 types of flowers and, as a result, 2 types of fruit. One type of flower is borne on long nodding stalks that rise from the bases of the upper leaves on the stems. Each stem bears 2–15 pale lilac to whitish flowers that are about ⅓–½ in. long. They open gradually and can usually be found from summer into early fall. The petals are curled inward along their midline and are rolled in about 1½ turns from the tip. These flowers produce flat seed pods (A) that look like peas and are 1–2 in. long. (These above-ground seed pods are not a food source.) A second set of flowers appears near the roots of the plant. They are tiny, greenish, lack petals, and are borne on thread-like, creeping stems. These flowers are self-fertilizing and they produce rounded, fleshy seed pods that contain a single, large, light-brown, peanut-like seed. The seed pods are covered with bristly hairs, are about ¼–½ in. in diameter, and are formed just beneath the surface of the ground or beneath the ground's covering of leaves and forest litter.

COLLECTION AND USE: The *seed* in the subterranean pods of Hog Peanut were a valuable source of food for the Indians of the central states, who collected them in quantity by raiding the burrows of small rodents. When they are fully formed in the fall, the seeds usually occur in a quantity sufficient for campers, if not whole tribes, and pilfering from mice is unnecessary. And digging up rodent burrows is probably more work than scraping up the barely buried seed pods from the base of the plant. The seeds can be eaten raw or cooked, and resemble fresh beans. The pods are leathery but crack free during boiling. Seeds can also be dried, roasted, and eaten like peanuts.

Seeds: nutmeat; cooked vegetable.

WOOD SORREL
Oxalis stricta and related species

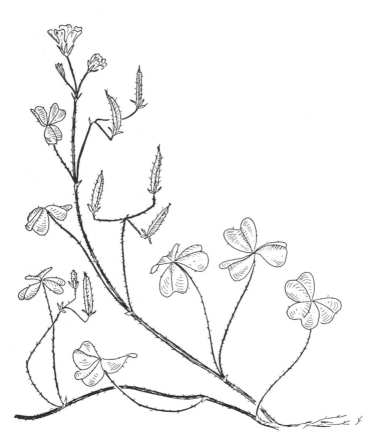

SIZE: 8–15 in. high
OTHER COMMON NAMES: Sour-grass,
    Sour trefoil, Lady's sorrel
HABITAT: Mainly in moist woods but
    also in dry woods and open soil
SEASON: Early summer through fall

IDENTIFYING CHARACTERISTICS: Wood Sorrel is a delicate woodland plant that is easily identified by its clover-like leaves and sour juice. The palmately compound leaves are at the ends of long leafstalks that alternate on stems in some species or rise directly from the ground in others. Each leaf is composed of 3 leaflets that are rounded and have a notch in their outer edge that gives the appearance of 2 overlapping leaves. The leaves and stems are soft and delicate and filled with a watery juice. The weak stems frequently sag toward the ground. The flowers are usually solitary and have spreading petals and 5 sepals. The flowers of *O. stricta,* one of the most widely distributed species, are yellow. In other species, flowers are white, pink, or violet.

COLLECTION AND USE: The sour, juicy foliage of Wood Sorrel has a refreshing, slightly thirst-quenching quality that has made it a favorite nibble of hikers and mountaineers. The *leaves* can also be used in salads, preferably mixed with other greens. Steeping the leaves in warm water will leach out some of the acid; cooled and mixed with sugar, the liquid makes a refreshing lemonade-like beverage.

CAUTION: The sourness of Wood Sorrel is due to oxalic acid. While small quantities of oxalic acid are present in a number of garden vegetables, including spinach, it is extremely poisonous in large quantities. High concentrations of oxalic acid are what make rhubarb leaves poisonous. As a result, Wood Sorrel can be a refreshing addition to the diet but should be eaten sparingly.

Leaves: trail nibble; salad; beverage.

SUMAC
Rhus typhina; also *R. glabra,*
R. copallina, and *R. trilobata*

SIZE: Bush or small tree, 4–15 ft. high
HABITAT: Dry, rocky, or gravelly soil of
  fields, clearings, and sometimes
  woods
SEASON: Midsummer through early
  winter

IDENTIFYING CHARACTERISTICS: The Staghorn Sumac *(R. typhina)* has smooth-barked branches that are covered with velvety hairs. The wood of the branches is orange with green streaks running through it; the core is large, soft, and pithy. Leaves are pinnately compound having 11–31 leaflets that are arranged opposite each other on the leafstalk. The leaflets have dark green upper surfaces and pale green and velvety undersides. They are from 3–5 in. long, are lance-shaped with pointed tips, and have serrated edges. In the early summer, flower stalks bearing clusters of small, unattractive, yellowish- or greenish-white flowers appear. The plants grow in clumps, some bearing staminate flowers and others pistillate. The mature pistillate clusters develop into dense, torch-shaped fruit clusters that range from 2–8 in. in length. The fruits are small, brilliant red, and covered with long red hairs. Ripe fruits remain on the trees throughout the winter. The Smooth Sumac *(R. glabra)* is similar to the Staghorn except that its branches lack hairs and have a bluish-gray appearance. The Dwarf or Wing Rib Sumac *(R. copallina)* is smaller and is found only on the East Coast. Its leafstalks have thin projections or wings between successive pairs of leaflets. The Squaw Bush *(R. trilobata)*, a species limited to the West Coast, runs 3–7 ft. high and has compound leaves with only 3 leaflets. All Sumacs can be easily spotted in the fall when their leaves turn a brilliant crimson or yellow. (*R. typhina* is illustrated.)

COLLECTION AND USE: The hairs on the *berries* of Sumac fruiting clusters are rich in malic acid—the same acid found in apples—which can be extracted to make a cool refreshing beverage similar to lemonade. The berries of Smooth Sumac, Squaw Bush, and Dwarf Sumac are more acidic than those of Staghorn Sumac but all can be used. Preparation is simple. Collect the entire ripe fruit cluster, preferably before heavy rains, which will wash away some of the acid. Bruise the berries slightly by rubbing the cluster through the hand and soak the berries in cold water until the solution is a pleasant pink color. (While hot water is faster, it leaches tannic acid from the berries and stems, leaving an unpleasant, bitter flavor.) Pour the mixture through a cloth or fine sieve to remove the berries, add sugar to taste, and chill. It may also be served hot like tea. Boiled Sumac berries are sometimes used as a remedy for sore throats.

CAUTION: The potent skin irritants poison ivy, poison oak, and poison sumac are all members of the *Rhus* genus. While these varieties share some similarities with the edible members of the genus, they are not easily confused: poisonous *Rhus* bear white fruits while the edible species all have brilliant red fruits.

Berries: beverage; medicine.

CASSINA AND INKBERRY
Ilex vomitoria and *I. glabra*

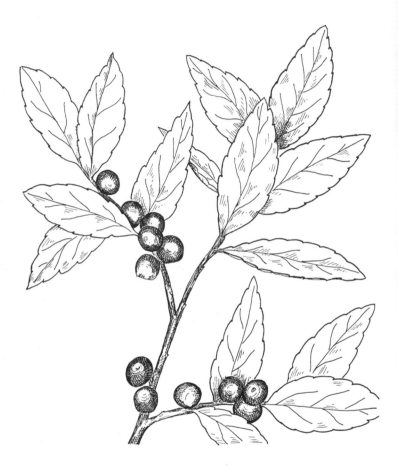

SIZE: Shrub or small tree up to 20 ft.
high

OTHER COMMON NAMES: Yaupon,
Gallberry

HABITAT: Sandy or peaty soil of woods
and clearings

SEASON: All year

IDENTIFYING CHARACTERISTICS: These are evergreen holly plants found mainly in the southeastern U.S. Cassina *(I. vomitoria)* has its northern limits in southern Virginia and northern Arkansas. It is a large shrub with thin, leathery leaves that are a deep green and shiny on their upper surfaces and a lighter, pale green underneath. The leaves are lance-shaped or elliptical and have rounded teeth around their edges that give them a scalloped appearance. The leaves are arranged alternately on the branches. The branches have whitish-gray bark. The small white flowers have either 4 or 5 petals and either 4 or 5 stamens. They are borne in small clusters that rise from the junctions of the leafstalks and branches. The flowers have very short stalks and appear to be attached directly to the branches. They are replaced by red berry-like fruits about ¼ in. in diameter; each contains between 4 and 9 small nutlets with grooves on one side. The Inkberry *(I. glabra)* is found over most of the same range as Cassina but extends much farther north along the coast (as far as Nova Scotia). It is similar to Cassina except that its flowers have either 6 or 8 petals and flower clusters are on long stalks; the berries are hard, dry, and black, and persist into winter; the nutlets are smooth. (*I. vomitoria* is illustrated.)

COLLECTION AND USE: Despite its repulsive specific name, which derives from the effect it had on Indians who engaged in ceremonial excesses, Cassina is one of the best tea substitutes among native North American plants. Unlike many of the plants that have been used as substitutes for tea, the *leaves* of Cassina and Inkberry contain significant quantities of caffeine to provide that slight physical stimulation most coffee and tea drinkers expect. The leaves may be gathered for use as tea at any time during the year. Before use they should be thoroughly dried over a slow fire or in an oven until they are almost black; otherwise the resulting beverage is unpalatable. The leaves are steeped in boiling water just like tea leaves. The resulting beverage has a pleasant flavor that is rather like tea but somewhat more aromatic.

Leaves: tea.

MAPLE
Acer; about 10 species

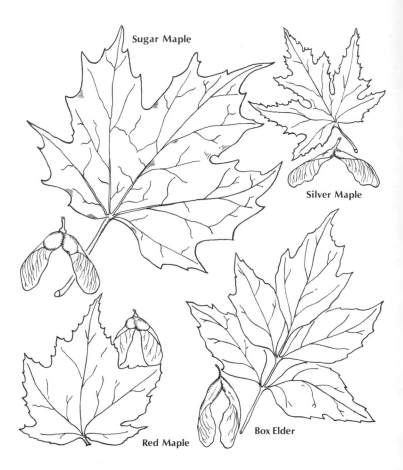

Sugar Maple

Silver Maple

Red Maple

Box Elder

SIZE: Large trees, up to 150 ft. high
HABITAT: Moist, cool woods
SEASON: Late winter, early spring

IDENTIFYING CHARACTERISTICS: All species of Maple produce sap that contains sugar but the amount varies from species to species. One of the better sugar producers and certainly the best known of the American Maples is the Sugar or Rock Maple *(A. saccharum),* which is also one of the largest North American forest trees. Its branches are widely spreading and the bark on old trees becomes deeply furrowed and grayish. The simple opposite leaves are palmately lobed, having 3–5 lobes. The leaves have long stalks and the blades are basically round with dark green upper surfaces and lighter undersides. The edges of the leaves are irregular with coarse, widely spaced teeth that are sharply pointed. The small flowers are yellowish-green and hang in clusters on long, drooping stalks. They appear at the same time the leaves begin to unfold and attach to the branches at the base of the leafstalks. The fruits ripen in the fall, and are conspicuous because of the 1–1½ in. long "wing." On the tree, 2 fruits are attached at their bases and hang from a single, long stalk. Other Maples are similar. The Red or Swamp Maple *(A. rubrum)* bears red flowers and the twigs have a reddish tinge. The leaves of the Silver, White, or River Maple *(A. saccharinum)* have whitish undersides (which look silvery in some light) and 5 lobes that are more deeply cut than those of the Sugar Maple. The only markedly different Maple is the Ash-leaved Maple or Box Elder *(A. negundo).* Instead of lobed leaves, the leaf is compound with 5 (occasionally 3 or 7) separate leaflets as if the lobes had been cut so deeply they became separate. The leaflets have coarse teeth and are sometimes slightly lobed.

COLLECTION AND USE: Although its importance has been diminished by the availability of cane sugar, the *sap* of the Maples—which flows from February to early April and, during thaws, even earlier—is a valuable sugar source. Sap flows best on warm, sunny days that have been preceded by cold, frosty nights. Trees are "tapped" by boring a ½ in. hole 3 in. into the trunk with a slight upward slant. A spile or spigot is fitted into the hole. Commercial spiles made from perforated metal can be obtained at hardware suppliers but equally good ones can be made by punching the pith out of 4-in. lengths of Elder (see p. 185), sharpening one end to allow sap to run into it, and cutting a notch in the other to hold pails or similar containers. Two spiles can be inserted in an average-sized tree, more in larger ones. Boiled over a fire in shallow pans, sap yields syrup; further boiling yields sugar. It takes about 3–4 gal. of sap to make a pound of sugar (a single large maple on a good day will often drip several times that amount). Sugaring is time-consuming, but the only real labor is collecting firewood; in a winter camp a fire is usually burning anyway and there are few better uses for its heat. The sap may also be drunk directly from the tree or used in cooking. If it is allowed to ferment a mild vinegar is produced (see p. 18).

Sap: sugar; vinegar; beverage.

JEWELWEED
Impatiens capensis and related species

SIZE: 2–4 ft. high

OTHER COMMON NAMES: Snapweed,
Touch-me-not

HABITAT: Forms patches in wet woods,
on creek banks, and near springs

SEASON: Spring and summer

IDENTIFYING CHARACTERISTICS: This is a smooth-stemmed annual that forms dense clumps in damp places. The erect stems are somewhat branched toward the top and exude a yellow-orange juice when broken. The leaves are alternate with an elliptical shape and range from 1–4 in. long. They have fine, regular serrations along their edges and prominent parallel veins that run from the midrib to the edges of the leaves. The flowers occur in groups of 2 or 3 on drooping branched stalks that attach to the stems just above the upper leaves. They are orange or yellow and sometimes are spotted with red or reddish-brown. The flower is curiously shaped: it has a long sac-like base that rather resembles a cornucopia and bends back on itself at its slender tip. The 2 petals are inserted in the open mouth of this horn. The common names, Snapweed and Touch-me-not, come from an interesting feature of the small, slipper-shaped seed capsules: when they are fully ripe, the gentlest touch causes them to burst open with a sharp snapping sound, violently expelling their several seeds.

COLLECTION AND USE: The *leaves and stems* of young Jewelweed shoots make an excellent potherb if they are collected in the spring when less than 6 in. high. They are tender and require little cooking. Despite Jewelweed's virtue as a spring vegetable, its best known use is as a field remedy for poison ivy. Auspiciously, Jewelweed favors the same habitats as the plant whose poison it counteracts and the two are often found growing together. If the sap from crushed leaves and stems is rubbed either on parts of the body that have come in contact with poison ivy or on parts that are likely to, the allergic symptoms are less likely to develop. An extract, made by boiling the plant in water, works even better but it will not keep. The extract also relieves itching in cases where symptoms have already developed. The plant will relieve itching from insect bites as well and it contains a fungicide that makes it a useful and effective treatment for athlete's foot.

Leaves and stems: potherb; medicine.

NEW JERSEY TEA
Ceanothus americanus

SIZE: Shrub, up to 3 ft. high
OTHER COMMON NAME: Redroot
HABITAT: Dry, sandy, or gravelly soil of
    open woods; also rocky banks
SEASON: Summer

IDENTIFYING CHARACTERISTICS: New Jersey Tea is a small shrub that is woody only near the base. Each year the soft flowering stems die back and are replaced the following year. The alternate leaves are oval with pointed tips and rounded or heart-shaped bases. They are dark green with lighter undersides and have 3 prominent veins that curve across the midrib and then arc toward the tip of the leaf. The leaves are from 2–3 in. long, have short stalks, and fine, blunt teeth around their edges. The white flowers are borne in clusters that resemble bunches of grapes. They are on long stalks that attach to the stems just above the leafstalks. The lower flower stalks are longer than those above and sometimes reach 8 in. in length. The plant is very conspicuous in flower, having between 2 and 10 flower clusters on each branch. The flower clusters range from about ½–1½ in. in diameter. The tiny individual flowers have 5 spreading petals that are curved inward and resemble claws. The roots are bright red.

COLLECTION AND USE: During the American Revolution when Oriental tea was under boycott, New Jersey Tea was one of the most popular substitutes, especially in regions running from New Jersey southward. In the more northern colonies, Labrador Tea (see p. 158) was the favored alternative. *Leaves* should be collected in the summer, preferably but not necessarily when the plant is in bloom, and dried. Drying can be done either in the sun, before a slow fire, or in an oven. The dried leaves should be used exactly like Oriental tea; the resulting beverage has a good flavor that approaches the genuine article although it is lacking in caffeine. The bright red *roots* of this plant can be used to prepare a dye.

Leaves: tea. *Roots:* dye.

GRAPE

Vitis Labrusca, V. aestivalis, and *V. rotundifolia*

SIZE: Large vines, often climbing high into trees

HABITAT: Moist soil of riverbanks and wet woods, also dry woods, thickets, and roadsides

SEASON: Fall, fruits; early summer, leaves

IDENTIFYING CHARACTERISTICS: There are about 2 dozen species of Grapes native to North America (all close relatives of the famous wine Grapes, *V. vinifera,* of Europe). However, grapevines in the wild grow very differently from their docile, cultivated relatives of vineyards and back gardens; wild grapevines frequently achieve enormous size. Grapes are woody vines that have loose, brown, papery bark that frequently hangs in strips from the older stems and can be pulled free in long shreds. They climb by tendrils that join the stems opposite the leafstalks. The leaves have long leafstalks, are arranged alternately on the stems, and are basically heart-shaped although they are frequently divided into a number of palmate lobes and have coarse, shallow teeth around their edges. Grapes bear elongated, branching clusters of fragrant, greenish flowers in the early summer. Like the tendrils, the flowers and the fruit are attached to the stems opposite a leaf. The grapes usually contain 4 hard pear-shaped seeds, although some will have fewer. Three species are both the best eating and the most common in North America. The Fox Grape, *V. Labrusca,* was the source of the popular cultivated Concord, Catawba, Chautauqua, and Champion strains. It is a high-climbing vine with clusters of grapes that are purple or purple-black and range from ½ to ¾ in. in diameter. The Summer or Pigeon Grape, *V. aestivalis,* bears black fruit between ¼ and ½ in. in diameter. The Muscadine, Southern Fox, or Bullace Grape, *V. rotundifolia,* is the ancestor of the Scuppernong Grape and has bark that is tightly attached and leaves that are shiny on both sides. Its purple grapes are ½–¾ in. in diameter.

COLLECTION AND USE: Because of the many species of Grape and the variation in the quality of the fruit, sample the fruit from a number of sources. The fruit forms only on the shoots of that season and young plants bear more heavily than old. If the *fruit* is sweet and pulpy, by all means eat it fresh, but if not, tart grapes that are mostly seeds can still make excellent jelly, conserves, pies, or juice. To make juice, simmer the fruit for about 20 min., strain out the skins and seeds, sweeten it to taste. When Grapes are mentioned, the first thing that usually comes to mind is wine. Depending on the Grape, fairly good wines can be made with experimentation. The *leaves* are also edible, having an enjoyable acid flavor that is imparted to foods wrapped in them during cooking. They are widely eaten as stuffed Grape leaves. The leaves should be collected in the early summer and can be stored for later use by packing in brine.

CAUTION: Grapes can be confused with the poisonous Moonseed (*Menispermum canadense,* see p. 213). However, Moonseed has a single cresent-shaped seed and it climbs by twining.

Fruit: fresh; jams and jellies; pies; beverage; wine. *Leaves:* wrapping for food.

MALLOW
Malva neglecta and
about 6 others

SIZE: 5–8 in. high
HABITAT: Waste areas, fields, and
    roadsides
SEASON: Spring, summer, leaves; early
    summer through fall, fruit

IDENTIFYING CHARACTERISTICS: While all species of the *Malva* genus can be used as food, the most widely recognized and most broadly distributed is the Common Mallow or Cheese Mallow *(M. neglecta).* It is a rather small plant that tends to recline so, despite its commonness, it is easily missed in the field. The leaves are rounded and vaguely heart-shaped with rounded teeth on their edges and slight broad indentations that suggest lobes. They range from 1–2 in. across and are on very long leafstalks that can reach 4–6 in. The leaves are arranged alternately on the stems. Flowers are borne in dense clusters at the junction of the leafstalks and the stems, where they hang from long stalks. They have 5 pale lilac or white petals. The fruits (A) are greenish-white and are tightly wrapped in the green leaf-like projections that formed the base of the flower. They are round and flat and look very much like miniature wheels of cheese. Plants continue to flower and bear fruit throughout the summer and fall until they are killed by early frosts.

COLLECTION AND USE: The Common Mallows of North America are closely related to the European Marshmallow *(Althaea officinalis),* the original source of the confection of that name. All *Malva* species have similar properties. The young *leaves* can be boiled in 2 waters and served as a potherb but, because they contain large quantities of the natural gums mucilage, pectin, and asparagin, they have a slimy character like okra that is distastful to many people. They may, however, be added to soups and stews to which they impart body and act as thickeners. The *fruits,* often known as cheeses, can be peeled free from their green covering and eaten in the field. They can also be boiled with the covering left on and eaten as a cooked vegetable or they may be added whole to soups and stews. A substitute for marshmallow can be prepared from the *roots* (not so good) or the fruits (better): cover the root or fruit with water and boil until the level is reduced by half. Cool, then beat the resulting viscous liquid into a froth resembling egg white. When beaten with sugar it is a reasonable field confection or it can be used as a substitute for meringue or whipped cream. The original uses of Marshmallow were medicinal, however. Water in which whole mallows have been boiled contains a substance that softens and relaxes the skin. Similar materials are the primary ingredient of skin lotions; this one is free. Taken internally, it is said to soothe and reduce internal inflammation, including sore throats. The leaves have been used in wound dressings to reduce inflammation.

Leaves: potherb; thickener; medicine. *Fruits:* cooked vegetable; confection; medicine. *Roots:* confection; medicine.

VIOLET
Viola; about 35 species

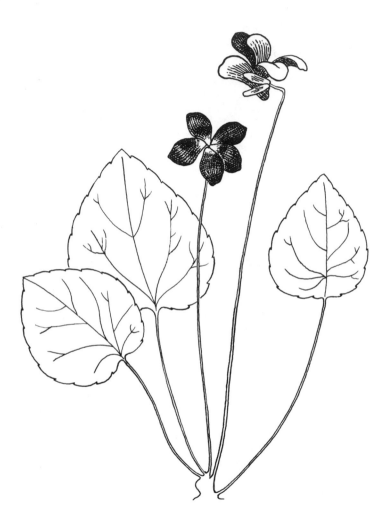

SIZE: 4–6 in. high
HABITAT: Dry and moist woods and
    fields, streambanks, swamps, and
    bogs
SEASON: Spring and early summer

IDENTIFYING CHARACTERISTICS: There are over 50 species of Violet growing wild in the U.S. with flowers that range from the typical violet-blue to yellow and white. For the person whose interest in these springtime flowers includes food as well as aesthetics, only those with blue flowers (about 37 species) are important. The dead giveaway in recognizing Violets is their flowers, among the first wildflowers to appear in the spring. A single delicate flower nods from the top of a 4–6 in.–long, very slender stalk that rises directly from ground level. About halfway up the flower stalk there are usually a pair of tiny leaf-like appendages. The flower itself has 5 petals. The petal that hangs down toward the ground is larger than the other 4 and is curled into a spur shape that cups the others. There are 5 stamens and the 2 lowermost ones have appendages that extend into the spur. These flowers almost never produce seeds, so picking them will not harm the plant. In the summer, Violets bear small, inconspicuous, fertile flowers that are self-fertilizing and never even get around to opening; they eventually form a drab seed capsule, sometimes underground. Violets also reproduce by stolons, or runners, in the same manner as Strawberries (see p. 123). While the flowers are remarkably consistent from species to species, the leaves are a different story. All rise directly from the rhizome, or underground stem, on long slender leafstalks that are 3–5 inches long, but the leaf blades vary from heart-shaped, to oval, to lance-shaped or arrowhead-shaped and some are so deeply notched that they look almost like compound leaves.

COLLECTION AND USE: Violet *flowers* are more well known for their beauty, fragrance, and medicinal uses than as food but they can be put to good use as food in a number of ways that preserve all these virtues. While it is hard to imagine making a meal of Violet flowers, and silly to do so, they make a refreshing trail nibble in the early spring. And if the herbalists, who claimed that violets cured and prevented bronchial disorders (they are very rich in vitamins C and A) and a host of other diseases, were right, they are also an excellent spring tonic. The beautiful color and smell of violets can be trapped in water by simply covering the blossoms with boiling water and letting them sit. Adding sugar (1 cup of extract to 2 cups of sugar) and bringing to a boil makes a syrup that has been used as a cough medicine and tonic. By treating the syrup as you would juice in making jelly with commercial pectin, a fragrant, violet-colored jelly can be made. The flowers can also be candied (once a popular confection) by dipping them in boiling sugar syrup, allowing them to dry, and rolling them in granulated sugar to eliminate the stickiness. The young *leaves* have a pleasant astringency and can be used as a salad green. They are best when mixed with other springtime greens such as Winter Cress (p. 112), Water Cress (p. 108), and Mustard (p. 104). The leaves can also be cooked as a potherb or added to soups or stews to add body.

Flowers: trail nibble; jelly; confection; medicine. *Leaves:* salad; potherb; thickener.

EVENING PRIMROSE
Oenothera biennis

SIZE: 3–5 ft. high

HABITAT: Dry open soil of waste areas, fields, and roadsides

SEASON: Spring, shoots; fall through spring, roots

IDENTIFYING CHARACTERISTICS: This biennial plant gets its name from its showy pale yellow flowers, which open in the cool of summer evenings. In its first year of growth, the plants form a rosette of many elongated, lance-shaped leaves that are 4–8 in. long and lie flat on the ground. They are all attached to the top of a stout, fleshy, branched taproot, have very short or no leafstalks, smooth edges that are sometimes slightly curly, and prominent midribs that are whitish or reddish. Tall flower-bearing stems that often exceed 5 ft. are formed in the second year. The stems are straight but may branch toward the top. They have a dense covering of smaller, alternate leaves with smooth edges that give the flower stems a fat, bushy appearance. The stems are sometimes tinged with purple and are covered with soft hairs. The flowers number from few to many and are borne in clusters at the top of the stems. They have 4 petals and 4 green leaf-like sepals that droop down below. The flowers are yellow when newly opened but may turn purplish as they grow older. They are between 1 and 2 in. in diameter. The cylindrical seed pods are pointed at the tip and are erect.

COLLECTION AND USE: During the first year, *roots* of Evening Primrose can be used as a cooked vegetable. They are best when collected from late fall to early spring; at other times they develop a peppery quality although boiling in several waters will remove most of it. (The easiest way to recognize the first-year plants is by the presence of nearby second-year plants with developed flower stalks.) The roots can be cooked by boiling or by roasting with meat. They can also be added to soups and stews. The young *shoots* in the spring of the second year can be used as a salad green but have a strong peppery quality. Small quantities mixed with bland greens make an acceptable salad.

Roots: cooked vegetable. *Shoots:* salad.

LABRADOR TEA
Ledum groenlandicum

A

SIZE: Shrub, about 3 ft. high
OTHER COMMON NAME: Bog tea
HABITAT: Bogs and wet peaty soils
SEASON: All year

IDENTIFYING CHARACTERISTICS: This is a northern plant that is common from Newfoundland to Alaska; in the U.S., it extends only into the northernmost states and then usually is found only in cold mountain bogs and forests. It is a small shrub with alternate, evergreen leaves that are lance-shaped and range from ¾–2 in. long. They are densely covered with a light brown wool on their undersides and have edges that are rolled inward. When crushed, the leaves yield a fragrant aroma. The flowers (A) are white and occur in clusters that resemble an inverted umbrella in which each rib is topped by a flower. The clusters are at the tops of the branches. The flowers have 5 spreading petals and between 5 and 7 stamens. Individual flowers are about ⅓ in. in diameter.

COLLECTION AND USE: The dried *leaves* of Labrador Tea were a popular substitute for Oriental tea when it became unavailable during the American Revolution. Before use, the leaves should be thoroughly dried in the sun or before a slow fire or in an oven. Preparation is the same as for tea and the resulting beverage has a pleasant aroma and a taste that reminds some people of Oriental tea. Unlike some wild tea substitutes, Labrador Tea is good served cold.

Leaves: tea.

WINTERGREEN
Gaultheria procumbens

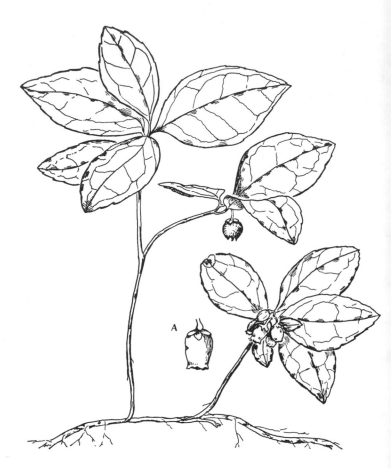

A

SIZE: 3–6 in. high

OTHER COMMON NAMES: Checkerberry,
    Teaberry, Mountain tea,
    Ivy-leaves

HABITAT: In infertile forests, particularly
    under evergreens

SEASON: All year, leaves; fall through
    spring, berries

IDENTIFYING CHARACTERISTICS: This tiny plant is actually a shrub with stems that creep along the surface of the ground or just below it. At intervals along the stem, leaf-bearing branches that look like individual plants thrust upward. They are from 3–6 in. high and have a distinct woody character. The shiny evergreen leaves are clustered at the top of the branches. The leaves have short leafstalks and are about 2 in. long. The blades are elliptical with points at both ends. The young leaves are fleshy and tender, pale yellowish-green with tinges of red or sometimes almost all red, and smell strongly of wintergreen when crushed; the older leaves are shiny, dark green with lighter undersides, have a tough leathery texture, and are less fragrant. In midsummer, the tiny, whitish bell-shaped flowers (A) hang from drooping stalks that join the stems at the bases of the leaves. The base of the flower eventually becomes fleshy and forms a red, berry-like fruit that is about ¼ in. in diameter. The fruit ripens in the late fall.

COLLECTION AND USE: The *leaves* of *G. procumbens* were the original source of oil of Wintergreen but were displaced by the twigs of Black Birch (see p. 65), which contains the same aromatic oil in larger quantities. Today, most wintergreen flavoring is prepared synthetically. The best way to enjoy the fragrance of this plant is in Wintergreen tea, which is prepared by steeping the leaves in boiling water. Fresh leaves are best because the oil is volatile and escapes upon drying. While Wintergreen leaves have been preserved by drying, the resulting beverage is usually weak. Some claim the potency can be increased by partially fermenting the berries in water, which is then heated for tea; this is impractical in the field. Both young leaves and *berries* are refreshing when eaten raw. The quality of the berries is improved by freezing, so they are at their best in the winter, when they can be found underneath the snow, or in the spring. Freezing causes them to swell and become more plump and juicy. Since the berries do not crush easily, a supply can be carried to eat on the trail. They are also good when added to pancakes and muffins. A beverage similar to root beer or wine can be prepared from a solution made by steeping the leaves in hot water (see p. 17). The leaves and berries contain a compound similar to aspirin that will reduce fever and allay minor aches and pains.

Leaves: tea; trail nibble; beer; wine; medicine. *Berries:* fresh; medicine.

BEARBERRY
Arctostaphylos uva-ursi

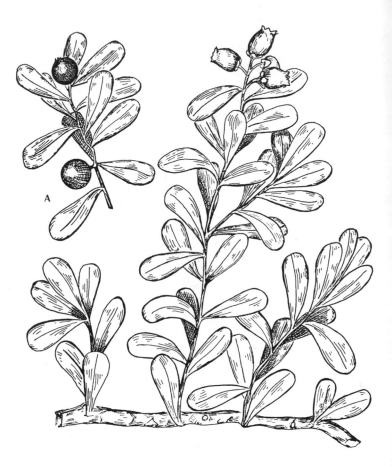

SIZE: Creeping shrub up to 6 in. high, about 4 ft. in diameter, forming mats

OTHER COMMON NAMES: Kinnikinick, Mealberry, Hog cranberry

HABITAT: Exposed rock and sand

SEASON: Fall, berries; summer, leaves

IDENTIFYING CHARACTERISTICS: Bearberry is an Arctic plant that is most abundant in the far north but extends southward into the United States. It remains mostly in the northeastern and central states, but can be found almost as far south as Mexico along the high ridges of the Rockies. The plant is a low creeping shrub that forms dense mats on the ground where it grows. The slender stems are woody, very flexible, and covered by loose, papery bark that is reddish or gray. The dark green, evergreen leaves are arranged alternately on small fleshy branches and are oblong to lance-shaped with pointed bases and rounded outer ends. They are about 1 in. long with very short leafstalks, and have a leathery texture. Between 5 and 12 densely clustered flowers hang from long stalks at the ends of the leafy branches. The flowers are urn-shaped and may be pink, white, or white with pink tips. The flowers are followed in the fall by clusters of dull red berries (A) about ⅓–½ in. in diameter that are almost filled by a single stone that is made up of 5–10 tiny, wholly or partially fused nutlets.

COLLECTION AND USE: The botanical name of this plant is rather emphatic: *Arctostaphylos* is the Greek and *uva-ursi* the Latin for "bear grape." The insipid, mealy quality of the *berries* makes them less than desirable as human food and, under normal circumstances, they'd be best left to the bears. However, in areas where they can be found in abundance, Bearberries can be an important survival food and cooking renders them more palatable although never to a point at which they could be called good. Still, a number of people have survived in the Arctic by eating boiled lichens, which are nutritious but yield a repulsive jelly. Bearberry does have other uses. Its *leaves* are the famous kinnikinick, a tobacco substitute prized by the northern Indians and used by generations of woodsmen. The leaves should be gathered in the summer months when they are milder than in the fall or winter, although they can be gathered the year round. They are dried, preferably in the sun (the process can be hurried by drying near a fire), and then crumbled and used like tobacco. Kinnikinick can also be mixed with tobacco when supplies begin to run low. The leaves, dried or fresh, can also be used to make a medicinal tea that is a mild diuretic said to be antiseptic to the urinary tract.

Berries: fresh(?). *Leaves:* tobacco substitute; medicine.

BLUEBERRY AND HUCKLEBERRY
Vaccinium, numerous species;
and *Gaylussacia,* several species

SIZE: Woody shrubs,
    3–7 ft. tall (Huckleberry);
    up to 15 ft. tall
    (Highbush Blueberry);
    5–20 in. tall (Lowbush Blueberry)
OTHER COMMON NAMES: Bilberry,
    Whortleberry, Deerberry, Hurts
HABITAT: Wet or dry sandy soil of
    woods and bogs
SEASON: Summer

IDENTIFYING CHARACTERISTICS: The common names Blueberry and Huckleberry are usually used interchangeably, but botanically they are two distinct groups. The fruit of the true Blueberries of the genus *Vaccinium* is filled with many soft seeds while the Huckleberry *(Gaylussacia)* fruit has 10 hard, seed-like nutlets. However, the appearance and taste of the fruits are so similar, that both frequently end up in the same picker's bucket. The Blueberries are divided into 2 groups, the Lowbush Blueberries and the Highbush species. Lowbush Blueberries are small woody shrubs, seldom reaching 20 in. in height. Typical of this group is *V. angustifolium,* also known as the Late Sweet Blueberry. It is a tiny shrub with very intricately branched stems. The branches are green, irregular, and bumpy and the leaves are alternate, bright shiny green on both sides, lance-shaped, and have tiny serrations around their edges. The flowers are white, bell- or urn-shaped, and about ¼ in. long. The blue berries range from ¼ to ½ in. in diameter and are covered with a powdery, whitish "bloom." This is a northern species found across the U.S. and extending far up into Canada. The fruit begins to ripen in August. A similar species, *V. vacillans,* the Early Sweet Blueberry, is found farther south, extending into Georgia. It looks much like *V. angustifolium* except that its branches and twigs are brownish and its oval leaves are pale green on top with whitish undersides. The berries are slightly smaller, darker colored with a whitish bloom, and begin to ripen in June. A typical Highbush Blueberry is *V. corymbosum,* known commonly as Swamp Blueberry. It is a tall bush that can reach 15 ft. in height and likes wet ground and swamps although it does sometimes grow in dry upland areas as well. It has elliptical leaves that are pointed at both ends and range from 1½ to 3 in. in length. They have smooth edges and have green upper surfaces and pale to whitish undersides. The berries begin to ripen in June. They are from ¼ to ⅓ in. in diameter, and bluish-black with a whitish bloom. The Huckleberries of the *Gaylussacia* genus are freely branching shrubs that often spread by underground stems to form clumps or thickets. They look very much like the larger Blueberry bushes but with more rounded oval leaves. The leaves of most species are covered with small dots of sticky resin on one or both sides. The berries range from blue to black, some having whitish blooms and others none, and contain 10 nut-like seeds. (*V. angustifolium* is illustrated.)

COLLECTION AND USE: There are few people who are at a loss about how to eat blueberries. Muffins, pies, tarts, jelly, and just plain fresh immediately come to mind. And a good patch of berries can easily supply enough *fruit* to take care of all of those uses for a year. The fruit is easily preserved by freezing (don't add sugar first; it toughens the berries) or by drying (outside in the sun it takes about a week). The Indians added the dried fruit to pemmican (see p. 14).

Fruit: fresh; pies; jelly; pemmican.

CRANBERRY
Vaccinium macrocarpon and *V. Oxycoccos*

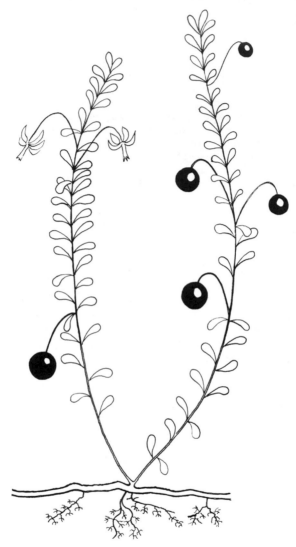

SIZE: Low creeping shrub, stems 6–24
      in. long
HABITAT: In bogs but sometimes in wet,
      peaty soil and around wet shores
SEASON: Fall and winter

IDENTIFYING CHARACTERISTICS: Cranberry is a low, ground-hugging evergreen shrub with branching, elongated stems that trail along the ground. Its leathery leaves lack stalks and attach directly to the stems. They are oval or oblong, ½–1 in. long, and alternate on the stems. The name *Cranberry* is a shortened version of "craneberry," the name given to this plant by early colonists because of the resemblance between the flowers and the head of the bird that bears that name. The red or pink flowers have 4 lance-shaped petals that curve backward to form a cup around the end of the flower stalk. The flowers have elongated, drooping stamens that look like the beak of a bird. The flowers hang from long bending stalks. In the fall, the flowers are replaced by bright red berries. Two major species of Cranberry can be found growing wild in the U.S. and Canada. *V. Oxycoccos,* known as the Small Cranberry, extends its range into the far north and it bears its flowers and fruit in clusters at the ends of its stems. The Large or American Cranberry, *V. macrocarpon,* has larger fruit and is the species that is usually cultivated in the U.S. It bears its flowers and berries in clusters located along its stems.

COLLECTION AND USE: That cranberry sauce is an indispensable accompaniment to the Thanksgiving turkey is a tradition born of the fact that the cranberry was one of the most-prized native *fruits* used by the early colonists. In fact, cranberries were held in such high regard that colonists in Massachusetts sent 10 barrels of the fruit to King Charles II as a gift. Besides their pleasant, tart flavor, they were valued because of their ability to keep for long periods of time without deteriorating. They withstand freezing and will stay fresh beneath winter snows—in fact, freezing seems to improve their flavor and they are at their best if collected after the first frosts in the fall. For home storage they can either be refrigerated for long periods or frozen. The fruit can also be preserved by drying, but unless storage for an indefinite period is called for, there is little point because it keeps so well on its own. Because of their sour tartness, cranberries are rarely eaten fresh but are usually cooked with sugar. They are best in sauces, jams, and jellies but also can be used in pies (often known as "mock cherry"), and the sweetened juice makes a refreshing beverage.

Fruit: jams and jellies; pies; beverage.

PERSIMMON
Diospyros virginiana

SIZE: Small tree, up to 60 ft. tall
HABITAT: Dry soil of woods, old fields, and clearings
SEASON: Fall and winter, fruit; summer, leaves

IDENTIFYING CHARACTERISTICS: The Persimmon is a small forest tree that sometimes reaches a height in excess of 60 ft. It is a close relative of the tropical ebony tree, and like that southern representative of its family, has very hard, blackish wood and dense, dark, and deeply furrowed bark. It has smooth, thickish leaves that are oval or oblong and come to a rather blunt point at the tips. They range from 3 to 6 in. long and are arranged alternately on the branches where they are attached by short, ½–1 in.–long leafstalks. Persimmon flowers in the early summer and bears 2 kinds of bell-shaped, pale greenish-yellow or cream-colored flowers. Sterile flowers are very small (about ⅜ in. across), usually grow in clusters of 2 or 3, and usually have 16 long tapering stamens. The fertile flowers are twice as large (between ½ and 1 in. across) and occur singly. These usually contain 8 stamens. The fruit, really a large berry, ripens after the leaves have fallen but does not attain its full sweetness until after frost. It contains several large flat seeds with a leathery outer covering. It is yellowish brown when ripe and generally ranges from 1 to 1½ in. in diameter.

COLLECTION AND USE: Persimmon has resisted attempts to market it because when it has attained full ripeness, it is so soft that it is almost impossible to ship. And there are few fruits that are more astringent and unpalatable than an unripe persimmon. Yet a properly ripe persimmon is one of the best tree fruits found in North America. The fruit clings tenaciously to the tree and can be collected well into winter. The easiest way to collect persimmons is to shake the tree: the fully ripe ones will fall to the ground. While the *fruit* can be eaten fresh and whole, the pulp is generally used for cooking. Since the ripe fruit is already a gooey proposition, preparing the pulp is no problem—simply put it through a colander to remove the seeds and skins. The pulp can be used immediately or preserved by canning or freezing. The pulp can be used to make a delicious bread (by substituting persimmon for banana pulp in a banana bread recipe), chiffon pies, and baked puddings. The high sugar content of Persimmon fruit gives it other uses as well. If equal parts of persimmon pulp and wheat bran (available at feed stores) are mixed together, spread onto baking sheets, and baked until fully dry, a malt-like substance, rich in sugar, results. After grinding this in a food mill, it can be used to make a substitute for molasses, beer, or vinegar. To make molasses, cover the ground mixture with boiling water, let it stand for about 12 hr., strain out the solids, and boil the liquid down to a syrupy consistency. For beer, steep about 3 lb. of the "malt" in 5 gal. of boiling water, strain out the solids, add brewer's yeast, and proceed as on p. 17. To make vinegar, ferment as for beer but when it starts to clear, add some commercial vinegar to inoculate it with the proper bacteria. The *leaves,* collected in the summer and thoroughly dried, make a tea that tastes rather like Sassafras tea.

Fruit: fresh; pies; sugar; beer; vinegar. *Leaves:* tea.

MILKWEED
Asclepias syriaca and *A. speciosa*

SIZE: 3–5 ft. high

HABITAT: In dry, well-lighted soil of roadsides, fields, and clearings

SEASON: Spring, young shoots; summer, leaves, flowers, and seed pods

IDENTIFYING CHARACTERISTICS: Numerous species of Milkweed exist and many are edible, but there are some western species known to cause livestock poisoning; hence, it is best to stick to the two described here. Both are very similar in appearance but *A. syriaca* extends throughout the eastern U.S. to the Mississippi River and *A. speciosa* from the plains to the West Coast. All parts of both plants contain a thick, sticky, milky sap that oozes freely when they are broken. Both have a stout unbranched stem that is covered with fine hairs, and leaves 4–8 in. long that are broad and fleshy with prominent veins and a stiff midrib. The leaves are oblong or oval and taper to a rounded point at both ends; they are joined to the stem in opposite pairs by short, stout stalks. The undersides are lighter in color and covered with fine hairs. The fragrant flowers are small, purplish to white, and located in clusters near the top of the stem. The clusters look like inverted umbrellas with a single flower attached to the end of each rib. The flowers have 5 upright, tubular projections, or hoods, each of which contains a tiny, finger-like projection, or horn. After flowering, Milkweeds bear green seed pods (A) that are about 4 in. long and covered with soft spines and hairs. When mature, they split open along one side releasing a great number of tiny seeds, each attached to a streamer of silk. (*A. syriaca* is illustrated.)

COLLECTION AND USE: Almost every part can be eaten, so Milkweed is a useful food source throughout the growing season. In spring, *young shoots* may be eaten raw or cooked like asparagus. They should be gathered while less than 6–8 in. high; otherwise they are tough and bitter. Young *leaves* can be collected from spring until flower buds form in summer. They are an excellent potherb but should be cooked in at least 2 changes of boiling water to remove the bitter principal, as should all other parts except young shoots. Unopened *flowers* and young *pods* are very good cooked vegetables. The unopened flowers can be collected through the summer and early fall. They have a dull, woolly appearance before cooking, but turn a bright green once boiled and look like broccoli. The pods should be collected before they become elastic when pressed with the fingers. When boiled the partially formed seeds and silk cook down into a delicate mass. The pods are somewhat mucilaginous, like okra; added to soups and stews, they act as a natural thickener. (Before adding, it's a good idea to cook them in one change of water to avoid giving the whole dish a bitter quality.) Drying the *sap* from leaves or stems in the sun or before a fire provides an acceptable substitute for chewing gum.

CAUTION: Take care not to confuse young Milkweed plants with the poisonous Dogbane (*Apocynum adrosaemifolium,* see p. 216). While it also contains a milky sap and has similar leaves, it is easily identified since its stems branch freely and lack hairs.

Young shoots: salad; cooked vegetable. *Leaves:* potherb. *Flowers and pods:* cooked vegetable. *Sap:* chewing gum.

WILD POTATO
Ipomoea pandurata

SIZE: Trailing and climbing vine; stems up to 12 ft. long

OTHER COMMON NAMES: Man of the earth, Mecha-meck

HABITAT: Dry soil of fields, roadsides, and open woods

SEASON: All year

IDENTIFYING CHARACTERISTICS: This vine prefers to grow along the ground but will climb where convenient supports are available. It has smooth, strong stems that branch frequently and often have a purplish color. The alternate leaves are of almost equal length and breadth and have sharp points and heart-shaped bases. Some of the leaves may be narrowed at the middle so that they have a fiddle shape. The leaves range from 1½–6 in. in length and have short hairs on both sides. The large showy flowers closely resemble those of the cultivated morning glory. They are bell-shaped with flared tops. The outside and flared part of the flowers is white but the inside of the tube is a reddish-purple. Stout flower stalks that are generally longer than the leafstalks rise from the stems at the bases of the leaves and bear from 1–5 flowers in branching clusters. The flowers are from 2–3 in. in diameter. The roots are enormous perennial taproots that extend vertically into the ground as deep as 3 ft.

COLLECTION AND USE: Wild Potato is difficult to dig but a single *root* can provide enough food for a long time. Roots have been recorded that exceeded 3 ft. in length and weighed more than 30 lb. The root looks like a gigantic version of its close relative the yam and, like that root, it is brittle and contains a milky juice when freshly dug. The Wild Potato can be prepared in any of the ways usual for potatoes. It is sweet but has a slightly bitter taste that is stronger in some plants than others. In the case of more bitter roots, boiling in more than one change of water helps. The roots are at their best from fall through spring, when they are filled with starch, but can also be used during the summer.

Roots: potato substitute.

MINT
Mentha piperita and numerous species

SIZE: Up to 3 ft. high
HABITAT: Moist soil of fields, meadows, roadside ditches, stream banks
SEASON: Spring and summer

IDENTIFYING CHARACTERISTICS: This large family includes such common herbs as sage, pennyroyal, basil, marjoram, and thyme as well as the true Mints, *Mentha*. Generally, members of the Mint family are characterized by square stems and opposite leaves containing aromatic oils. Beyond that, because of the ease with which the species form hybrids, identification is difficult for any but the experienced botanist. The simplest solution is to rely on the sense of smell. Unless a hiker has no sense of smell whatsoever, it is extremely unlikely that a patch of Mint he has crushed with his feet will go by unnoticed; if it does, it is probably so lacking in fragrance that it isn't worth bothering with anyway. Two of the best known wild Mints are Spearmint *(M. spicata)* and Peppermint *(M. piperita)*. The leaves of Spearmint are lance-shaped and usually attach directly to the stem although plants are occasionally found on which the leaves have very short stalks. The leaf blades taper to a sharp point and are narrowed at the base. The edges of the leaves are unevenly serrated. Flowers are in dense terminal spikes and range from purple to white. The leaves of Peppermint have short leafstalks, are narrower than those of *M. spicata,* and have even serrations on their edges. Flowers are purple and are in looser spikes. The only species native to North America (*M. arvensis)* has serrated leaves on stalks and purple flowers that are borne in small compact clusters located on the stems at the attachment points of the upper pairs of leaves. (*M. piperita* is illustrated.)

COLLECTION AND USE: The fragrant *leaves* of the Mints have familiar uses that are scarcely worth enumerating. One use that is relatively unfamiliar, except in Arab countries, is as a salad green. Because of the fragrance of the leaves, many people prefer to mix them with other greens. The leaves also make an excellent tea when steeped in boiling water; they can be used as flavorings for jellies and sauces, and as a seasoning for almost anything, particularly meat. The leaves preserve their flavor when dried and can be used in this form for tea or seasoning.

Leaves: salad; tea; seasoning.

GROUND CHERRY
Physalis pubescens and related species

SIZE: 6–24 in. high; some to 3 ft.
OTHER COMMON NAMES: Husk tomato,
    Strawberry tomato
HABITAT: Dry or moist open woods,
    roadsides, waste areas, and
    recently cultivated ground
SEASON: Late summer and fall

IDENTIFYING CHARACTERISTICS: These are plants closely related to tomatoes and potatoes (and to the poisonous members of the Nightshade family) that are native to the southern states through to the tropics. Originally ornamental plants, they have escaped from cultivation and can be found throughout the U.S. The fruit (A) is so distinctive that there is no danger of confusing the *Physalis* species with poisonous relatives. It is a smooth, many-seeded and tomato-like yellow-green berry about ½ in. in diameter that is completely enclosed within a thin, papery husk that looks like a Chinese paper lantern with 5 sides. The husk is between 1 and 2 in. long; in the various species it ranges from pale yellowish-white to bright orange. The husks hang from long stalks that are attached to the stems at the bases of the leaves. The berry is joined to the husk at the top in the same position that a lightbulb would occupy in a lantern. Depending on the species, the stems may be either branched or unbranched and are sometimes covered with fine hairs. The leaves are alternate, dark green, pointed, and, in most species, have coarse irregular teeth around their edges. The flowers (B) are usually borne singly on long drooping stalks that are attached to the stems at the bases of the leaves although in some species clusters of 2–5 are found. They are bell-shaped and range in color from white to yellow and often have a darker colored center. (*P. heterophylla* is illustrated.)

COLLECTION AND USE: The fruits fall to the ground before they are fully ripe; as the husk dries out, they rapidly become sweet. Unless the *berries* are completely ripe, they have a strong and unpleasant flavor. Since they reach full ripeness off the plant, the berries can be picked before they fall and left in their husks until they turn a rich yellow. Berries left in their husks will keep for weeks without spoiling. Ripe Ground Cherries can be eaten where they are found in the field and have a pleasant flavor and texture. They can also be eaten with additional sweetening and cream. When cooked they make excellent sauces, preserves, jams, and pies. A preserve can be made simply by boiling the berries in a heavy sugar syrup; to make jam it is necessary to add commercial pectin for jelling. Crushed cooked berries mixed with raw onion, spices, chili peppers, sugar, and vinegar make an excellent relish.

Berries: fresh; jam; condiment; pies.

BROOKLIME

Veronica americana;
    also *V. beccabunga*
    and *V. Anagallis-aquatica*

SIZE: Sprawling stems up to 3 ft. long
HABITAT: Swamps, muddy streambanks,
    and shallow water
SEASON: Spring and summer

IDENTIFYING CHARACTERISTICS: Brooklime is a semiaquatic perennial that frequently grows on muddy banks in places where Water Cress is also found. Like Water Cress, it has sprawling stems that lie flat along the surface of the ground or water. It is, however, a larger plant with stems that can be 3 ft. in length and sometimes even longer. Its stems also resemble Water Cress in that they are jointed and roots are sent out from the lower joints to keep it anchored in the soft, muddy soil in which it grows. The fleshy leaves of *V. americana,* American Brooklime, are basically lance-shaped but tend to be wider at the base, giving them a slightly triangular appearance. They are arranged on the stems in opposite pairs and attach to the stems by short leaf-stalks. They are from 1 to 3 in. long and about half as wide with coarse teeth around their edges. European Brooklime *(V. beccabunga),* which has become established in the Northeast, has leaves that are broader and slightly shorter than those of the American species. Another closely related species, *V. Anagallis-aquatica,* known as Water-Speedwell or Brook Pimpernel, has leaves that attach to the stems without leafstalks and that have smooth edges or edges with very indistinct teeth. The Brooklimes bear large numbers of tiny blue or pale lilac flowers that are arranged along a long flower stalk that rises from the stems where the uppermost pairs of leaves are attached. The flowers have 4 petals and 2 long stamens that hang out. After flowering, the seeds are formed in a flattened and rounded capsule that is notched at the top and is divided by a furrow into halves.

COLLECTION AND USE: The European Brooklime made it into herbal lore as a preventative for scurvy and other malnutritional diseases and our species undoubtedly possess similar properties. But medicinal properties aside, the *leaves and stems* of Brooklime make an excellent salad green with a mild astringent quality. Not only does it sometimes grow with Water Cress, but its acidity complements Water Cress's pungency when the two are mixed in a salad. Cooked for a short time in boiling water, Brooklime is also an excellent potherb. For both uses, the tenderest part of the plant is the growing end of the stem with its smaller leaves. It should be collected in the early spring and summer before the flower stalks appear. Although the larger leaves toward the base of the stems are not as tender, they can be snipped off all summer and cooked as a potherb, even though they are no longer suitable for salads.

CAUTION: Like other aquatic plants, Brooklime should be disinfected before eaten raw if there is any doubt about the purity of the water it is growing in or near. Harmful bacteria can cling to the stems and are not removed by washing. The plant can be effectively sterilized by washing in water containing a dissolved water purification tablet of the type sold in camping stores (see p. 3).

Leaves and stems: salad; potherb; medicine.

CLEAVERS
Galium aparine

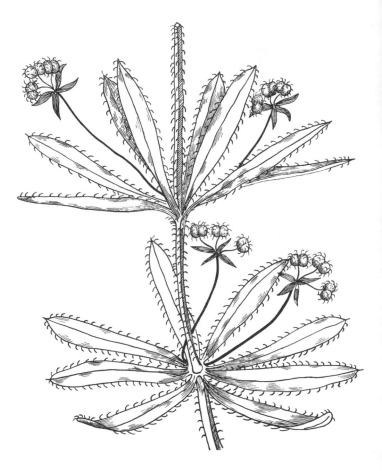

SIZE: Reclining stems 1–3 ft. long
OTHER COMMON NAME: Goosegrass
HABITAT: Damp shaded ground of rocky
    woods, thickets, and sea coasts
SEASON: Spring, young sprouts; early
    summer, fruits

IDENTIFYING CHARACTERISTICS: An inconspicuous plant that grows among the dense foliage of woodland thickets, Cleavers' weak reclining stems are supported by surrounding plants and it usually blends in very well. Still, it grows so profusely over its wide range that the person who looks for it is almost certain to find it. The annual stems are distinctly 4-sided and have small stiff bristles along the corners that point backward and allow the plant to cling to nearby supports. At intervals of several inches along the stem there are whorls of 8 elongated lance-shaped leaves that lack leafstalks and are rounded toward the base and tipped with a stiff bristle. They are from 2–3 in. long and have backward-pointing bristles along their edges and midrib. The point on the stems where the leaves attach looks like a swollen joint and is covered with fine hairs. At each joint in the stem, 2 flower stalks that exceed the length of the leaves attach just above the leaves and are situated opposite each other. Toward the tips of the flower stalks, there is a whorl of 4 tiny leaves; just above this the stalk splits into 3 branches, each bearing a tiny greenish-white flower. Flower stalks bearing 1 or 2 flowers also occur. The flowers are followed by 2-lobed dry fruits that are equipped with the same reversed bristles and are spread by clinging to passing animals.

COLLECTION AND USE: Cleavers is a member of the same family as the coffee tree and is probably the closest North American plant in aroma and flavor to that commodity although it is sadly lacking in caffeine. The *fruits* should be gathered in the early summer (June and July in most areas) and roasted in an oven or over a slow fire until they are dark brown. After roasting, they should be crushed, and then preparation proceeds as for coffee. When collected in the spring, the tender *shoots* make a potherb that requires little cooking. Cooked and cooled, shoots can be dressed and eaten in a salad. Cleavers was formerly much eaten in weight-reducing diets. Because of the many bristles on the foliage, a mass of Cleavers *leaves and stems* makes a very efficient improvised strainer for use in the field.

Fruits: coffee substitute. *Shoots:* potherb; salad. *Leaves and stems:* strainer.

HIGHBUSH CRANBERRY
Viburnum trilobum

SIZE: Shrub or small tree up to 12 ft.
   high
OTHER COMMON NAMES: Cranberry tree,
   Pimbina
HABITAT: Cool woods, shorelines,
   thickets, and rocky slopes
SEASON: Late summer and winter

IDENTIFYING CHARACTERISTICS: This large shrub or small tree has branches that are covered with grayish-brown bark and leaves arranged in opposite pairs on the branches. The leaves have stalks that are ⅓–1 in. long and blades that are nearly round in general outline. They are palmately lobed and veined, with 3 lobes, and have coarse pointed teeth around their edges except toward the bases of the leaves. The general shape of the leaves is suggestive of Maple leaves. The flowers are in clusters that are about 2–4 in. in diameter and are located at the ends of the branches. The clusters are composed of 2 types of flowers: flowers around the edge of the cluster are large and showy and have 4 white petals; in the center of the cluster are a great many tiny white flowers of similar appearance. The outer flowers are sterile while the inner ones are fertile. In the fall, fruits are borne in flat-topped clusters at the ends of the branches. The berry-like fruits first become orange and finally turn bright red when they are fully ripe. They are about ⅓ in. in diameter and contain a single disk-shaped stone that is smooth and ungrooved.

COLLECTION AND USE: Although the Highbush Cranberry is not related to the cranberry of the stores (genus *Vaccinium* of the Heath family), its acid *fruit* has a similar quality and is used as cranberries in some parts of the country. The berries can be collected in the fall but are improved by freezing; since they hang on the branches all winter, they can be collected later. Birds do eat the fruit but generally leave it alone until early spring when other sources of food have been exhausted. The fruit is generally too sour to be eaten fresh, but cooked with sugar it resembles cranberry sauce. However, the seeds are large and should be strained out. Boiling the fruit with sugar and lemon or orange peel and juice, and then straining, produces a juice that is rich in vitamin C and can be diluted and used as a beverage. The juice can also be made into a beautiful clear jelly of excellent flavor. Commercial pectin is required. The juice can also be fermented into wine.

CAUTION: A European species, the ornamental Snowball bush *(V. opulus),* has escaped from cultivation in some areas. It looks exactly like *V. trilobum,* and some botanists consider the native American species to be a variety of the European species. The only difference between them is that the fruit of *V. opulus* is too bitter to be palatable.

Fruit: jelly; beverage; wine.

ELDER
Sambucus canadensis
and *S. melanocarpa*

SIZE: Shrubs, 5–12 ft. high
HABITAT: Rich, moist soil of stream
    banks, ditches, and woods
SEASON: Summer, flowers; late summer,
    fruit

IDENTIFYING CHARACTERISTICS: The two species of Elder are very similar in appearance; *S. canadensis* predominates in the East and *S. melanocarpa* in the West. In areas where Elder grows in abundance, it often forms impenetrable thickets because of its habit of sending up erect stems from a tangled mass of roots. The young stems have greenish bark covering a narrow cylinder of wood that surrounds a core of soft, white pith. In older stems the bark becomes grayish-brown and the woody layer thickens. The opposite, pinnately compound leaves have 5–11 leaflets that are arranged in opposite pairs on the leafstalks. The leaflets are elliptical to lance-shaped with pointed ends and sharp serrations along their edges. Elder is most conspicuous when it is in flower. The white flowers are borne in flat, circular clusters that are often 5–8 in. in diameter. Individual flowers are about ¼ in. in diameter and are shaped like 5-pointed stars. The flowers are replaced by clusters of small, purplish-black berries containing 3 tiny seed-like nutlets and a rich wine-colored juice. (*S. canadensis* is illustrated.)

COLLECTION AND USE: Elderberries are one of the easiest fruits to gather because the *berries* are in dense clusters that can be easily broken free and the berries pulled off over a suitable container. The fruit is produced in great abundance—Elder plants are frequently bent from their weight. Elderberries produce a wine that is excellent, but there are numerous other uses. While the berries lack an acid "tartness," and thus are of poor quality raw, they have an excellent flavor that is brought out by cooking with other tart fruits such as lemons or oranges; the acid juice of Sumac may also be used (see p. 141). Fruit to which acid has been added can be stewed and eaten or used as a basis for a superior jelly if pectin is added. The fresh fruit may be added to pancakes or muffins or used as pie filling. The preferred way to make pies is with dried fruit and Elderberries take very well to drying; the flavor of the dried fruit is often considered to be superior to that of the fresh berries. Dried berries can be used in winter to make pie filling, sauces, or juice (if boiled in a lot of water). The *flower clusters,* called Elder Blow, can be coated with batter and fried as fritters, or made into a fragrant wine. Individual flowers are good in muffins and pancakes or may be steeped for tea (alone or with Mint). The easily hollowed *twigs* make good spiles to tap Maple and other sap trees. (They also make flutes, whistles, and pea shooters.)

CAUTION: Some species of Elder have bright red berries. These are unpalatable and may be poisonous. They should not be eaten.

Berries: wine; jelly; pies; beverage. *Flowers:* wine; flavoring; tea. *Twigs:* spiles; musical instruments.

SWEET GOLDENROD
Solidago odora

SIZE: 3–4 ft. tall
HABITAT: Dry, sandy soil of fields and
    open woods
SEASON: Summer and early fall

IDENTIFYING CHARACTERISTICS: Of the more than 60 Goldenrods of the genus *Solidago* found in the U.S., only one *(S. odora)* has use as a food plant. Unlike the others, Sweet Goldenrod's leaves contain an aromatic substance with a fragrant anise-like scent that is released when the leaves are crushed. If the plant looks right, and the anise smell is present, you probably have Sweet Goldenrod. This plant is a stout perennial that sends up a single, 2–3 ft.–long, unbranched stem from a system of fibrous roots. Unlike most other Goldenrods, which have serrations around the edges of their leaves, the leaves of Sweet Goldenrod are smooth-edged. The elongated (about 4 in. long by ½ in. wide), lance-shaped leaves alternate on the stem and attach directly to it without leafstalks. When the leaves are held up to the sun or a bright light, they can be seen to be dotted with translucent spots. The yellow flowers are borne in a loose cluster at the top of the stem. They are situated along the top surfaces of a number of long branching stems that are usually slightly recurved.

COLLECTION AND USE: The generic name, *Solidago,* is derived from the Latin words *solidus* and *ago.* Translated literally it means "to make whole," but loosely it means "to heal," for this plant has long been credited with medicinal properties. The dried *leaves* are steeped in water to make a pleasant herbal tea that can also be used as a change of pace or substitute for other beverages in the field. Preparation involves picking fresh leaves in the summer, drying them thoroughly either in an oven or the sun, and storing in sealed jars. Sun-drying is the best method because too much heat will drive off most of the aromatic oil. Storing in tightly sealed containers will also help preserve the pleasant anise scent as will avoiding bruising the leaves when picking them and then crumbling the dried leaves just prior to use. Sweet Goldenrod, as well as the other Goldenrod species, is the host of an insect that forms *galls* at the tops of the stems. The gall is a round swelling in the stem that when cut open reveals a tiny worm. In the winter, Goldenrod stems remain upright and many will have a gall toward the top. In the absence of other types of fish bait, and in an emergency, the worm inside can be pressed into service.

Leaves: tea. *Galls:* fish bait.

JERUSALEM ARTICHOKE AND SUNFLOWER
Helianthus tuberosus and other species

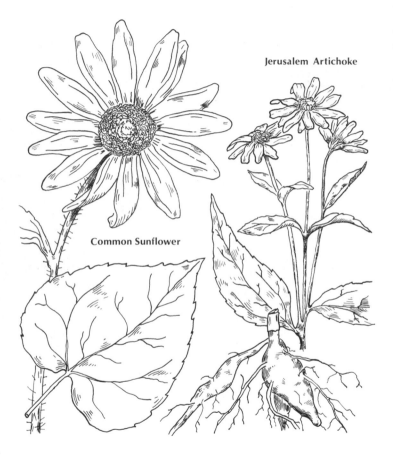

Jerusalem Artichoke

Common Sunflower

SIZE: 3–10 ft. tall
HABITAT: Open ground in dry soil;
   fields, clearings, and roadsides
SEASON: Fall and spring, tubers; late
   summer and fall, seeds

IDENTIFYING CHARACTERISTICS: Sunflowers are another of those confusing groups of plants in which fine distinctions between species are best left to the botanists. Taken together they may be identified by their flowers, which are typical of all plants in the Composite family. What looks like a single flower is really a dense cluster, or head, made up of a great many minute flowers that have been modified into two types: ray and disk flowers. Flowerheads may be composed of one or both types. A daisy flower is a good example of the two types combined: around the outside are "petals," which are ray flowers; the "button" at the center consists of disk flowers. The flowerheads of the Sunflowers have ray flowers that are always yellow and disk flowers that range from dark brown to purple or yellow. Some species of Sunflowers produce seeds in sufficient quantity to be useful as food, for example, the Common Sunflower *(H. annuus).* It is a coarse annual plant that often reaches 6 ft. in height. It has alternate leaves with definite leafstalks. The leaves are oval in shape, rough to the touch, and have toothed edges. The flower heads are very large, often reaching 6 in. across, and the disk, where seeds are produced, is flat and 1–2 in. across. One species, the Jerusalem Artichoke *(H. tuberosus),* is a perennial that develops edible tubers. It grows to 10 ft. but is more slender and branching than the Common Sunflower. It has leaves similar to those of the Common Sunflower but narrower and more pointed. It grows in dense clumps in the wild and bears many flowerheads 2–3 in. in diameter. The disks of the flowers are small, rounded, yellow, and do not produce quantities of edible seed.

COLLECTION AND USE: When Sunflowers are filled with sufficient quantities of large ripe *seeds* to make gathering them worthwhile, the heads should be collected and allowed to dry until the seeds are easily freed. They are best roasted and eaten like nuts. They can also be used as a source of meal or oil. When the seeds are crushed and placed in water, the hulls float to the top and can be removed. Drain the water, then dry the meats and grind into meal. Boiling the water mixture drives off a light, sweet-smelling oil that is excellent for cooking. The oil, which is about 20% of the weight of the seeds, can be skimmed off the surface of the water after it is allowed to cool. Jerusalem Artichoke was formerly cultivated for its *tubers,* which have a soft, watery texture and a sweetish taste. They are shaped like sweet potatoes, grow to 3–5 in. long, and can be eaten raw in salads, partially cooked and pickled, or boiled and roasted like potatoes. They are very digestible and said to be more nutritious than potatoes.

Seeds: nutmeats; oil; flour. *Tubers:* salad; pickles; potato substitute.

COLTSFOOT

Tussilago farfara;
  also *Petasites palmatus*
  and related species

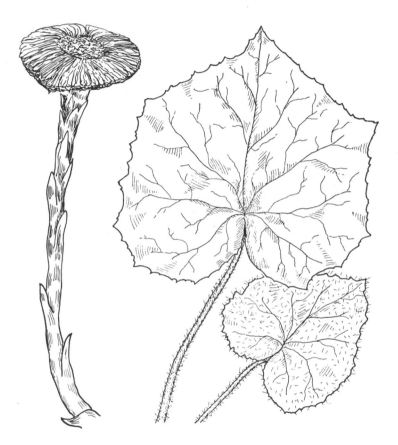

SIZE: Flower stems 4–18 in. high; leaves
     about 6 in. high
HABITAT: Damp soil of stream banks,
     woodlands, and clearings
SEASON: Spring and summer

IDENTIFYING CHARACTERISTICS: The two genera of Coltsfoot are very similar in appearance. The species of the *Petasites* genus are native North American plants and the single representative of the *Tussilago* genus, *T. farfara,* was introduced from Europe and is found from Newfoundland south to Pennsylvania and West Virginia and inland to Minnesota. Coltsfoot flowers in the early spring before its leaves appear. In the spring, the creeping perennial rootstock sends up a 4–18 in. high flower stalk that is covered with small, leaf-like appendages that clasp the stem. Those of *T. farfara* are tightly wrapped around the stem, giving it the appearance of a young stalk of asparagus, while those of the *Petasites* species are looser so that the stalk has a somewhat bushy appearance. The typical Composite flowers (see p. 189) have several rows of ray flowers surrounding a center of disk flowers. *T. farfara* bears a single yellow flowerhead that looks very much like a Dandelion flower; *Petasites* bears numerous purplish-white flowerheads that are densely clustered at the top of the stalk. After the flowers have gone to seed and the flower stalks wilted, the leaves appear. They are large, 2–6 in. wide, and have long leafstalks that rise directly from the ground. When young they are covered with a dense wool that persists on the undersides of mature leaves. The leaves of *T. farfara* are heart-shaped with coarsely toothed edges; those of *Petasites* vary somewhat but in most species they are kidney-shaped and cut into a number of prominent lobes with sharply toothed edges. (*T. farfara* is illustrated.)

COLLECTION AND USE: The use of the European Coltsfoot *(T. farfara)* as a remedy for coughing is probably older than medical records. Its long popularity was probably due in no small part to its pleasing flavor, which has also been used in flavoring candies. The flavor can be extracted by boiling the *leaves* in water. The flavored water can then be mixed with sugar and used as a cough syrup or in making hard candies. The dried leaves can be used to make a fragrant tea or smoked like tobacco. The young leaves of the *Petasites* species make a good potherb. Coltsfoot leaves also provide a substitute for salt: roll the leaves into balls and dry them before the fire; when thoroughly dry, burn them. The resulting ash is very salty and can be used in the wilderness to season food.

Leaves: medicine; flavoring; tea; tobacco substitute; potherb; salt substitute.

BURDOCK
Arctium lappa and related species

SIZE: 2–6 ft. high
HABITAT: Waste areas and roadsides; in moist soil
SEASON: Spring, young leaves and shoots; summer, stalks and roots

IDENTIFYING CHARACTERISTICS: This is the familiar plant that bears those tenacious round burs that are so adept at fastening themselves to clothing. Its alternate leaves are very large, often 2 ft. long and 1 ft. wide, and have stout stalks with deep furrows along their length. They are heart-shaped, dark green, and covered by many interconnecting veins in a net-like pattern. Because of the size and shape of the leaves, young plants resemble rhubarb. Since Burdock is a biennial plant, it is not until its second year of growth that it puts forth a tall branching stem that bears flowers followed by the seed-carrying burs. The tiny purple flowers are in rounded heads that are about 1 in. in diameter. The heads occur both in clusters or singly at the ends of the branches of the flower stem. (*A. lappa* is illustrated.)

COLLECTION AND USE: Despite Burdock's reputation as an obnoxious weed, it is the source of several very palatable foods. For use as a *root* vegetable, first-year plants (those lacking flower stems) should be selected since the roots of second-year plants are too fibrous to be much good. Even the roots of first-year plants are tough if dug much after midsummer. Burdock has a deep taproot so it cannot be pulled from the ground; a small shovel is necessary to gather the roots. The rind should be pared off the roots and the white core cooked in 2 changes of water, the first containing a little bicarbonate of soda to break down the fibers. The pithy core of the second-year *flower stems* can be prepared in the same way but care must be taken to peel away all the bitter green rind or the flavor will be affected. The remaining white pith is tender and juicy and makes an excellent vegetable. It can also be eaten raw with oil and vinegar as a salad. The pith of the *leafstalks* can be eaten in the same ways. The very young *leaves* can be used as a salad green or boiled in at least 2 changes of water as a potherb.

CAUTION: Because of Burdock's resemblance to rhubarb, the leaf blades of which are poisonous, care should be taken if use as a potherb is intended. Rhubarb leaves lack the net-like vein pattern that characterizes Burdock and are very smooth and shiny, whereas those of Burdock are slightly woolly and rough.

Roots: cooked vegetable. *Stems:* cooked vegetable; salad. *Leaf stalks:* cooked vegetable; salad. *Leaves:* salad; potherb.

THISTLE
Cirsium vulgare and related species

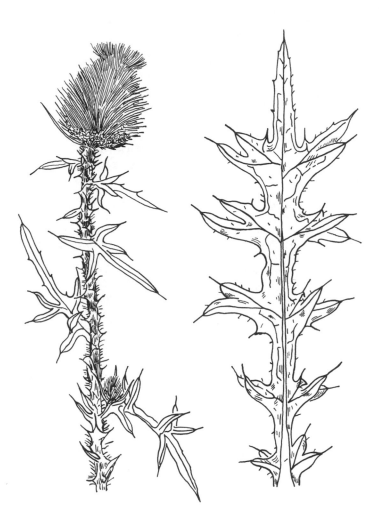

SIZE: Up to 5 ft. high when flowering
HABITAT: Clearings, meadows,
    roadsides; other species virtually
    everywhere
SEASON: Spring through fall

IDENTIFYING CHARACTERISTICS: The Thistle is a very familiar plant to anyone who has walked unaware into a patch of them and run afoul of their spiny leaves. And it is the presence of spines on the edges of the leaves that makes Thistles extremely easy to identify. As a group, Thistles are either annual, perennial, or biennial plants having leaves that lack leafstalks and are usually divided into deep, opposite lobes with coarse teeth that have sharp, stiff spines at their tips. A few species, however, have leaves that lack lobes and have only spine-tipped teeth. The Composite flowerheads (see p. 189) are borne either singly or in clusters at the top of a flower stem that bears alternate leaves smaller than those clustered at the base. In some species, the stem itself is covered with sharp spines. The flowerheads are fairly large and made up of a great many minute tubular flowers held in a vase-like green cup composed of many green appendages resembling leaves; some may have spiny tips. The flowerheads look like brushes and are usually purple but may be yellowish or white. One of the most common Thistles is the Hog Thistle *(C. vulgare).* It is a biennial with toothed, spiny leaves, a flower stem with spines along its length, and purple flowerheads that are about 2 in. high and 1 in. in diameter. The flower stem reaches a height of 5 ft. (*C. vulgare* is illustrated.)

COLLECTION AND USE: Like nettles, if you can get beyond their defenses Thistles are a good food plant. And because they are so distinctive and readily recognized and grow in such a diversity of habitats over virtually all of North America, they are an ideal survival food. Aside from the fierce spines, Thistle foliage is tender and mild-flavored although some species are better than others. The *leaves* can be used as a potherb and make a good salad green if the spines are removed, but the work involved is too much for most people. A better food is obtained from the *stems.* Stripped of their leaves, peeled, cut into short sections, and boiled, they make a cooked vegetable of excellent quality. The tough fibers of the stems can be twisted into a strong twine. The *roots* can also be eaten either raw or cooked. First-year roots are the best but even then flavor is flat and not particularly good. They are nutritious and could be important if survival is the objective.

Leaves: potherb; salad. *Stems:* cooked vegetable; thread. *Roots:* cooked vegetable.

CHICORY
Cichorium intybus

SIZE: 2–3 ft. high when flowering

OTHER COMMON NAMES: Blue sailors, Succory

HABITAT: Waste areas, fields, and roadsides; prefers clay soils

SEASON: Spring, leaves; fall to spring, roots

IDENTIFYING CHARACTERISTICS: The leaves of this plant are mostly clustered in a rosette at the top of a deep, perennial taproot. They are oblong, taper toward the base, and are deeply divided into opposite pairs of lobes with coarse irregular teeth around their edges. They look very much like Dandelion leaves but are less delicate and have leafstalks and midribs with a purplish cast. They range from 3–6 in. in length. In the early summer, a single, rapidly growing flower stem develops from the center of the leaf cluster. The stem is rather stiff with short branches and may reach 4 ft. in height. It is covered with short stiff hairs and much smaller, clasping leaves alternate along its length. The bright blue flowerheads are attached directly to the upper part of the stems. They are typical of the Composite family (see p. 189) and resemble those of the Dandelion but have a somewhat ragged appearance. The flowers are open in the morning, generally closing by noon except on very cloudy days.

COLLECTION AND USE: In the spring, the very young *leaves* can be gathered and used as a potherb. Since they look very much like Dandelion leaves (particularly when they are newly opened) and can be used at the same time, they are often gathered with Dandelion greens. Their taste when cooked is similar—they are bitter and should be boiled in more than one change of water; unless gathered at a very early stage, they become too bitter to use even then. They may also be used as a salad green. In Europe, roots are kept in the dark where they will form an abundant cluster of crisp white leaves that are used in salads under the name *Barbe du Capucin*. For a substitute in the field, cut the young leaves free from the root as far beneath ground level as possible. The blanched underground portions of the leaves make a superior salad with a flavor that resembles endive, a close relative. Probably the best known use of Chicory is as an addition to, or substitute for, coffee. For this purpose the *roots* are dug (preferably in the autumn, winter, or early spring), washed clean of earth, and roasted before a slow fire or in an oven until they are brown all the way through. They are then ground and brewed like coffee. The resulting beverage is stronger than coffee and somewhat more bitter but is one of the better wild coffee substitutes. Many people like to add it to coffee, claiming it makes a fuller, richer brew.

Leaves: potherb; salad. *Roots:* coffee substitute.

SALSIFY AND GOAT'S BEARD
Tragopogon porrifolius and *T. pratensis*

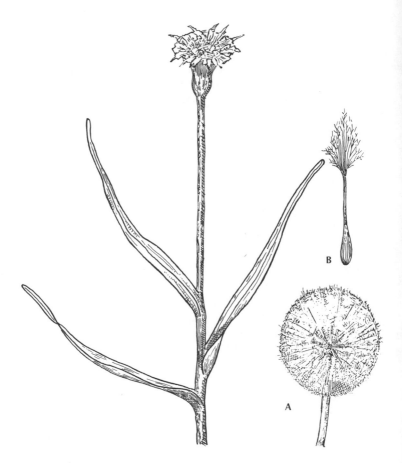

SIZE: 1–3 ft. high

HABITAT: Open areas, fields, and
roadsides

SEASON: Spring to fall, roots; spring,
leaves

IDENTIFYING CHARACTERISTICS: These are biennial plants with large tap-roots and tape-like leaves up to 1 ft. long that look like blades of grass and contain a milky juice. In their first year, the leaves are clustered in a rosette at the top of the taproot. The plants flower in the second year, sending up a tall stem with smaller leaves that wrap around it at their bases and are arranged alternately. The flowers look like oversized Dandelion heads (see p. 200) and are yellow in Goat's Beard *(T. pratensis)* and purple in Salsify *(T. porrifolius).* When they are ready to shed their seeds (A), the heads become round fluffy balls similar to those on the Dandelion. Each seed (B) is attached to a plume of branched silk threads that suggest a goat's beard, hence the common name. (*T. porrifolius* is illustrated.)

COLLECTION AND USE: Salsify is cultivated as a garden vegetable in some parts of the U.S., but was once much more popular and escaped from cultivation, spreading widely. The *roots* of the wild plants, while smaller than the cultivated variety, are an acceptable source of food. Only first-year roots should be used, as they become unpalatable after the flower stem appears. They are prepared by boiling in 2 changes of water preferably with a pinch of bicarbonate of soda added to the first. The roots can also be roasted until dark brown before a slow fire or in an oven, ground, and used as a substitute for coffee. When the top of the root is cut off about 3 in. below ground level, the resulting *leaf crown,* including the bases of the leaves and stems, makes an excellent cooked vegetable that can be used throughout the spring and summer. It is tender and requires very little cooking.

Roots: cooked vegetable; coffee substitute. *Leaf crowns:* cooked vegetable.

DANDELION
Taraxacum officinale and related species

SIZE: 3–5 in. high; flower stems to 15 in.

HABITAT: Grassy open places, fields, and waste areas

SEASON: Spring, leaves; early summer, flowers; spring to fall, roots

IDENTIFYING CHARACTERISTICS: The Dandelion is so familiar it needs little description. Its leaves are oblong, narrowing toward the base, and are cut into irregular, opposite lobes with edges covered with coarse, irregular teeth. The slender leaves are clustered in a rosette at the top of a deep, sometimes forked, perennial taproot. The bright yellow flowerheads are typical of the Composite family (see p. 189), being made up of a great many minute flowers of the ray type. The flowerheads occur singly on hollow stems that contain a milky juice. On cloudy days the flowerheads remain tightly closed (A). The flowerheads mature into silky balls (B) that release wind-borne seeds, each attached to a streamer of unbranched silk threads.

COLLECTION AND USE: The best known use of Dandelions is as an early spring green vegetable; it has long been in favor because of its reputed medicinal properties. This reputation is not without basis: Dandelion is very rich in vitamin A. Unless the *leaves* are gathered early in the season and properly prepared, they are very bitter. They should be cooked in at least 2 changes of boiling water and as the season progresses longer cooking and more changes of water are required. As soon as the flower stems appear, they are generally too bitter to be eaten no matter how much they are cooked. The crisp white leaves that have been blanched by growing in the dark (by transplanting roots into a cellar or covering plants outside) make an excellent salad. In the field, a good substitute for this delicacy is obtained by cutting the top of the root 2–3 in. below ground level to free the cluster of leaves. The top of the root and the bases of the leaves that are white from being underground can be sliced into salads or cooked as a vegetable. This part is not bitter, so long cooking is not required. The *roots* when dug in the early spring, peeled, and cooked in 2 changes of water (with a little bicarbonate of soda added to the first) make a good root vegetable that is in a class with turnip, parsnip, and Salsify. The roots may be used throughout the year as a coffee substitute. They should be roasted before a slow fire or in an oven until they are completely dry and dark brown throughout. After grinding, they are used just like coffee. The resulting brew is somewhat stronger than coffee but of good flavor. About 1 teaspoon is sufficient for a cup. The *flowers* can be used to make a delicate, flowery wine.

Leaves: potherb; salad. *Roots:* cooked vegetable; coffee substitute. *Flowers:* wine.

WILD LETTUCE
Lactuca canadensis and *L. Scariola*

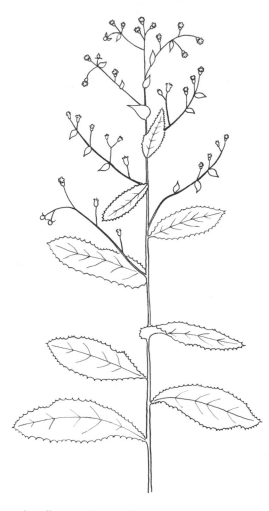

SIZE: 1–5 ft. tall, sometimes taller, at
maturity; eaten when less than 1
ft. tall

OTHER COMMON NAMES: Horseweed,
Prickly lettuce, Compass plant

HABITAT: Fields, roadsides, clearings,
and borders of woods

SEASON: Spring and early summer,
before flowering

IDENTIFYING CHARACTERISTICS: While these coarse, rather large plants are close relatives of our cultivated lettuce *(L. sativa)* and one of them *(L. Scariola)* is generally believed to have been the ancestor of the garden varieties, it is only when they are very young that they bear any resemblance to the plants that we usually know as lettuce—and to many eyes, even that may be pushing things a bit. The most readily spotted feature that they have in common with cultivated lettuce is that when the leaves and stems are broken they ooze a milky juice, hence the generic name *Lactuca.* Both species of Wild Lettuce found in the U.S. are classed as biennials but both will occasionally flower and seed in their first year of growth. Of the 2 species of Wild Lettuce, one, *L. canadensis,* also known as Horseweed, is a native plant; and the other, *L. Scariola,* which is known as Prickly Lettuce or Compass Plant, sneaked in from Europe. In its first year of growth, the native plant consists of a rosette of 5–12 in.–long leaves that rise directly from the top of a taproot at ground level. They are usually deeply notched and toothed so they look very much like oversized Dandelion leaves (see p. 200). In its second season of growth (or in the first if it can't wait), it sends up a single flower stalk 2–8 ft. tall. The flower stalk bears alternate leaves along its length, the ones toward the bottom are usually notched and toothed but gradually become lance-shaped with smooth edges toward the top. A loose, branching flower cluster is formed at the top of the stem. The flowers are all of the ray type (see p. 223) and are yellow when they open but sometimes become purple or blue with age. The European interloper has leaves that are basically oblong, deeply notched, and also look rather like Dandelion leaves. The leaves have backward projections on their bases that clasp around the stems. A unique feature of the leaves that accounts for this plant's being known as the Compass Plant is that they tend to twist at their bases so that their edges are vertical and aimed at the sun. Both the stems and the midribs of the leaves are covered with weak spines. The flowers are borne in clusters and look like those of *L. canadensis.*

COLLECTION AND USE: Despite their rather superficial and apparently coincidental resemblence to cultivated lettuce, Wild Lettuce plants are an excellent wild vegetable. The *leaves* can be used as a salad green but only when they are very young, in the early spring. By the time they are 5 in. or so in length, they begin to develop a bitterness that gets progressively stronger as the plants mature. When the flower stalks appear, they are far too bitter to be used in salad and can be used as a potherb only if cooked in several changes of water. The young leaves, however, make an excellent delicate potherb that requires very little cooking. No water need be added to a pot; simply fill a pan with washed leaves, cover, and cook over low heat for a few minutes. The spines of *L. Scariola* present no problem, as they soften completely in cooking. These plants are said to have medicinal properties and when eaten in large quantities have a mild tranquilizing effect.

Leaves: salad; potherb; medicine.

Poisonous Plants

As far as the common poisonous plants are concerned, modern men are probably more ignorant than people living in the Dark Ages, although the comparison is somewhat unfair considering that they were frequently put to use in those days. The fact is, each year there are numerous fatal cases of plant poisoning and many more cases that are treated by physicians. A knowledge of poisonous plants is as essential to survival in the wild as a familiarity with edible ones.

Included in this brief section are those plants that are most easily confused with edible species as well as those that are deadly and should be familiar to anyone who proposes to collect and eat wild plants. While there are other poisonous plants, many are so uninviting that few would attempt to eat them. Also not included here are the common skin irritants, poison ivy and poison oak and poisonous (as well as edible) mushrooms.

This section should not be taken as a warning not to collect edible plants; however, it is important that the wild-food eater be aware that dangerous plants do exist and know how to avoid them.

☠ HORSETAIL

Equisetum hyemale
and numerous related species

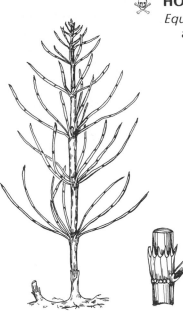

SIZE: 1–3 ft. high
OTHER COMMON NAMES: Scouring rush,
    Pipes, Joint grass, Foxtails
HABITAT: Damp to moist soil of
    swamps, stream banks, woods,
    and fields

Horsetails are primitive, rush-like plants with deep perennial stems or rhizomes and erect above-ground stems that are either branched or unbranched. The stems are divided into definite sections with closed ends that pull apart easily at the joints. Each joint is covered with a sheathing membrane (A) that is composed of a number of fused leaves. The sections of the stem are cylindrical, usually hollow between the joints, and have a series of fine grooves along their length. In some species thread-like branches that look like leaves radiate from the joints of the stems. The rind of the stems contains gritty particles of silica. A cone-like fruiting body (B) is borne at the top of the stem. The stems contain a toxin that has caused cases of livestock poisoning, but cases of human poisoning are rare. This is not a plant that many people would think of attempting to eat, although very young shoots have been mistaken for asparagus; people have eaten the pulp of peeled stems in small quantity without ill effect. It is a useful plant to know, however. Because of the silica in the rind, a ball of stems makes an excellent scouring pad for camp cookware or a substitute for sandpaper.

☠ FLY POISON
Amianthium muscaetoxicum

A

B

SIZE: 1–2 ft. high
HABITAT: Low sandy soil of bogs and
    open woods

Fly Poison is an extremely toxic plant with a bulbous root that is layered like that of an onion and could be mistaken for one of the wild *Allium* species (see p. 50). However, its lack of the characteristic onion smell easily separates it from that group of plants. It has tape-like leaves that are usually between ½ and 1 in. wide and are attached to the stem just above the top of the bulb. The single, smooth stem supports an elongated cluster of whitish-green flowers (A) with 6 petal-like segments that remain on the plant and turn green or purplish as they grow older. The flowers are followed by seed pods (B) that have 3 sharp, horn-like projections and are filled with elliptical seeds that have a fleshy, red coating. Both the foliage and root of this plant are toxic. Hands should be carefully washed after handling it: cases of poisoning caused by touching hands to the mouth have been reported.

☠ DEATH CAMASS
Zigadenus; a number of species

A

SIZE: Various species, 1–4 ft. high
OTHER COMMON NAMES: Poison camass,
    White camass, Crow poison
HABITAT: Sandy pinewoods and bogs,
    limestone gravels, meadows, and
    prairies

This is another poisonous plant that somewhat resembles the Wild
Onions of the *Allium* genus (see p. 50). It has a layered bulb and thin
grass-like leaves that rise from the top of the bulb. The leaves are
creased along the midrib so that they have a V-shaped cross section.
A single stem grows up through the cluster of leaves and bears small
white to greenish or pink flowers (A) on lateral stalks along its upper
part and small leaves lower down. The flowers have 6 petal-like
segments with 1 or 2 shiny gland-like spots at the base. While this
plant lacks the characteristic smell of onions, it has a pleasing appearance and no offensive odor, so that experimentation is tempting.
However, it contains a potent alkaloid that causes vomiting, diarrhea,
and death in many cases.

☠ FALSE HELLEBORE
Veratrum viride

SIZE: 2–3 ft. high at maturity
OTHER COMMON NAMES: White
    hellebore, Indian poke, Itchweed
HABITAT: Swamps and low areas

While it is unlikely that this plant would be confused with edible species, it often grows abundantly in the same habitats occupied by Marsh Marigold and Water Cress; unless care is taken, it can be accidentally mixed with those greens. It contains a nerve toxin that causes a slowing of the heart rate and a lowering of blood pressure. In the spring, False Hellebore pushes a tightly rolled cluster of leaves above the ground. It is at this stage that it is most easily collected inadvertently. The mature plant consists of a single stem with many large oval leaves alternating along its length. The leaves lack leafstalks and clasp the stem; they have a series of longitudinal pleats or corrugations that are also obvious in the young sprouts. The yellowish-green flowers are borne in dense, elongated clusters at the top of the stem in midsummer.

☠ BLUE FLAG
Iris prismatica and related species

SIZE: 8–24 in. high
HABITAT: Brackish, salt, or fresh water
    marshes; sandy shores and
    meadows; swamps, bottomlands,
    and forest borders

The leaves and underground stem of the Wild Iris contain an irritating substance that, if ingested, causes digestive upsets. The main danger to the collector of wild foods is confusing it with Sweet Flag, or Calamus (see p. 48), or with young Cat-tail (see p. 38). The tape-like leaves of Blue Flag resemble those of both plants. Confusion is only a problem when flowers are lacking. Blue Flag bears typical Iris flowers on single unbranched or branched flower stems (depending on the species). The rootstock looks rather like those of Calamus and Cat-tail, but it lacks an odor and has a strong, unpleasant taste; whereas the roots of Calamus have a pleasant odor and taste, and those of Cat-tail, while odorless, have a rather bland, "swampy" taste.

☠ BOUNCING BET
Saponaria officinalis

SIZE: 1–2 ft. high
OTHER COMMON NAME: Soapwort
HABITAT: Waste areas, roadsides, and
    ditches

The toxic principal of Bouncing Bet is a substance of a class of com-
pounds called saponins. They are natural soaps and the mucilaginous
juice of this plant will form suds when mixed with water. In fact, the
crushed green plant can be used as a wilderness soap substitute.
However, when this plant is eaten, severe irritation of the digestive
system results. The plant has a single unbranched stalk with opposite
pairs of leaves located at intervals along its length. The leaves are
lance-shaped or elliptical and have smooth margins and longitudinal
veins. They lack leafstalks and their bases wrap around the stem so
that it often appears as if the stem passes through the center of a single
double-pointed leaf. Several much smaller, less developed leaves are
on short branches that rise from the stem directly above the point of
attachment of the larger leaves. The large rose-colored flowers are
borne in flat-topped clusters that are attached to the stems just above
the topmost pairs of leaves. The flower consists of a tube formed by
the fusion of 5 sepals enclosing 5 petals with free tips that spread out
above the tube.

MOONSEED
Menispermum canadense

A

SIZE: Climbing vine
OTHER COMMON NAME: Yellow parilla
HABITAT: Rich thickets, stream banks, and woods

This is a poisonous plant that strongly resembles wild and cultivated grapes in both foliage and fruit. The purplish-black fruit form in clusters that are the same shape as grapes; the fruit about the same size as wild grapes, grow in the same habitats, and ripen at about the same time. But where grapes have a number of small seeds, Moonseed has a single flattened, cresent-shaped seed (A). The leaves look very much like grape leaves, particularly when both are not available for comparison. However the stems do not get as woody as those of the grape, nor do they develop a covering of loose, papery brown bark as do mature grape vines. Also Moonseed climbs by twining while grapes have tendrils that twine around supports.

☠ HORSE CHESTNUT
Aesculus glabra and related species

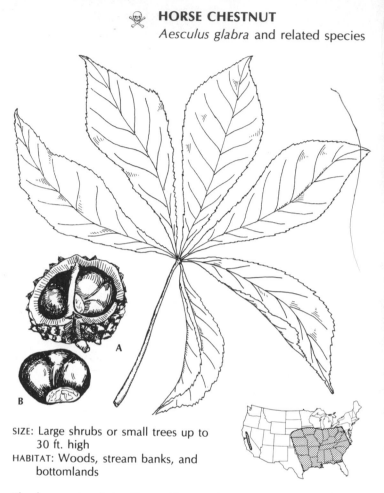

SIZE: Large shrubs or small trees up to 30 ft. high

HABITAT: Woods, stream banks, and bottomlands

The large nuts of the Horse Chestnut have a starchy meat and a tempting appearance, but they contain a toxic substance that acts on the nervous system. The nuts were used as food by some tribes of Indians but only after long leaching to remove the poison. When necessary to survival, crushed nuts and twigs stirred into ponds or pools intoxicate fish and cause them to float to the surface although use of fish poisons is usually illegal. The oppositely arranged leaves are palmately compound having 5–7 elliptical to lance-shaped leaflets that are attached to the leafstalk at a common point. The fruit is a spiny greenish capsule that contains 1–3 large nut-like seeds (A); these are brown and have shiny, leathery shells and a large scar on one side. The green husk often falls away as the seeds ripen. The seeds are slightly kidney-shaped (B), about 1 in. in diameter, and about 1½ in. long.

☠️ **POISON HEMLOCK**
Conium maculatum

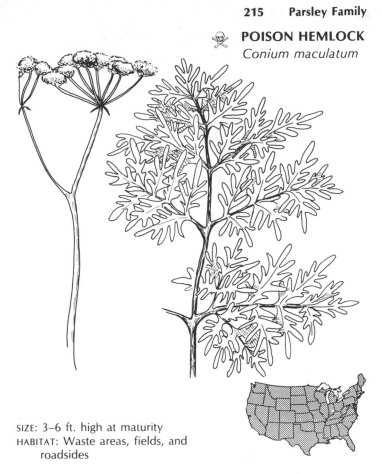

SIZE: 3–6 ft. high at maturity
HABITAT: Waste areas, fields, and
    roadsides

Poison Hemlock was introduced into North America from Europe and is closely related to the native Water Hemlock. It is as effective a killer as Water Hemlock but its mechanism of poisoning is different. While Water Hemlock causes fatal convulsions, Poison Hemlock produces a paralysis that results in death when the muscles controlling breathing cease to function. Poison Hemlock is not related in any way to the hemlock tree; the tree is not poisonous and its needles can be used to make tea. The plant bears a superficial resemblance to other members of the Parsley family, especially wild carrot, known as Queen Anne's lace, but it has smooth leafstalks while those of Queen Anne's lace are covered with hairs. Poison Hemlock has tall, stout, branching stems that are often covered with spots. The leaves are pinnately compound but are divided several times (i.e., leaflets that are themselves compound leaves, etc.). The leaflet blades are also deeply divided and have a feathery, fern-like appearance. It has a fleshy white taproot and white flowers that are borne in umbrella-like clusters at the top of the stems.

☠ WATER HEMLOCK
Cicuta maculata and *C. bulbifera*

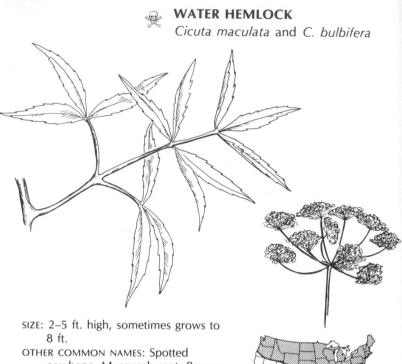

SIZE: 2–5 ft. high, sometimes grows to 8 ft.

OTHER COMMON NAMES: Spotted cowbane, Musquash-root, Beaver poison

HABITAT: Swamps, stream banks, and wet, low ground

This is a deadly plant. A single bite of its roots, which resemble parsnips in both appearance and flavor, is sufficient to kill a man and a small quantity of young foliage accidently included in potherbs or salad greens collected from swamps or wet ground can cause serious poisoning. As a member of the Parsley family, it is a close relative of many of our food plants including parsley, chervil, coriander, caraway, dill, fennel, parsnip, and carrot (which also grows wild and is known as Queen Anne's lace), and, unfortunately, it resembles many of these plants. What sets the *Cicuta* genus apart from other plants in this family is the vein pattern on the leaflets. The secondary veins on the lance-shaped leaflets of the 3-parted pinnately compound leaves branch from the midrib and run out toward the edge of the leaf where they branch and end in the notches between the teeth on the leaf's edge; in all other genera the veins end at the points of the teeth. Other identifying characteristics include roots that are finger-like and clustered, yellow lines crossing the pith of the bases of the stems that are evident when the stem is cut lengthwise (in older plants the yellow lines become walls separating air chambers in the stem), and whitish flowers borne in umbrella-like clusters at the ends of erect stems.

☠ DOGBANE

Apocynum androsaemifolium
and related species

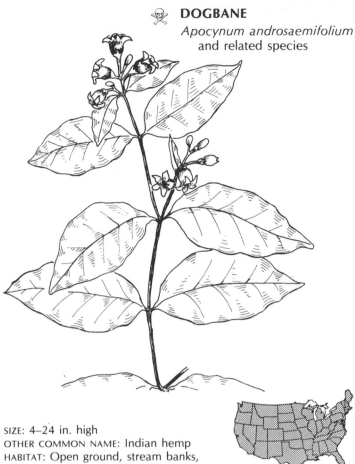

SIZE: 4–24 in. high
OTHER COMMON NAME: Indian hemp
HABITAT: Open ground, stream banks,
    and borders of woods

The Dogbanes bear a superficial resemblance to the Milkweeds (see p. 170), particularly the young plants. They have opposite oval leaves with dark green, smooth upper surfaces and paler undersides that are covered with fine hairs. The stems contain a milky juice, as do those of Milkweed, but they branch whereas those of Milkweed do not. The stems are completely smooth and covered with a tough fibrous rind. Milkweed stems are covered with hairs. The pink flowers are bell-shaped, ¼–½ in. in diameter, and are borne in loose-spreading clusters located along the stems as well as at the tops of the stems. The Dogbanes have been pinpointed as the cause of numerous cases of poisoning, but the actual mechanism of their toxicity is still undetermined. They are related to oleander, which is so toxic that an oleander stick used as a skewer for outdoor cooking has been known to cause fatal poisoning.

☠ JIMSON WEED

Datura Stramonium, D. metaloides, and *D. Metel*

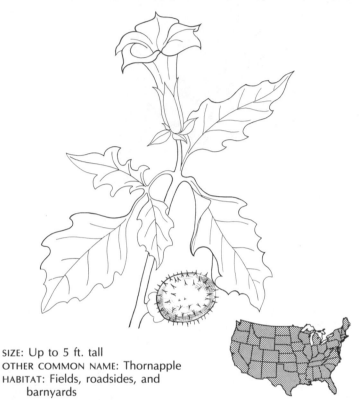

SIZE: Up to 5 ft. tall
OTHER COMMON NAME: Thornapple
HABITAT: Fields, roadsides, and
    barnyards

While this coarse, unpleasant-smelling plant is extremely difficult to think of in terms of food, it is so common and so poisonous that it is one that everyone who picks wild plants for food should know. Jimson Weed is a 2–5 ft.-tall weed with a stout, hollow stem. The smooth green leaves have very large coarse teeth around their edges and may be 4–6 in. in length. In young plants they have been mistaken for spinach! The plant bears showy white or violet flowers throughout the growing season. They are trumpet-shaped, several inches long, and look a lot like petunias. They attach to the stems where they fork and are supported by a stout, erect stalk. The other often-used common name, Thornapple, comes from the characteristic fruit—a spiny green oval 1½–3 in. long that rests at its base on a papery disk. Both fruit and flowers are present at the same time and all parts of the plant are poisonous. Jimson Weed contains alkaloids that are related to belladonna. Poisoning symptoms start with an unquenchable thirst and dilation of the eyes, proceed to delirium and hallucination, and in cases of severe poisoning, to convulsions and coma.

Illustrated
Glossary
and Index

Illustrated Glossary

Alternate. Refers to leaves and other plant parts (buds, etc.) that occur singly on the stems rather than in pairs or groups.

Annual. A plant that flowers, fruits, and dies in one growing season.

Basal. Parts of the plant located at, or very near, ground level.

Biennial. A plant that lives for 2 years, growing only foliage in its first year and flowering and fruiting in its second.

Blade. The flat, expanded part of a leaf.

Bulb. An underground food-storage organ composed of modified leaves wrapped tightly around a section of the stem. Cutting a bulb in half reveals a number of layers. An onion is a bulb.

Calyx. The outermost and lowest parts of a flower. It is composed of sepals and is usually green (see diagram, p. 224).

Catkin. A dense, finger-like flower cluster consisting of many minute flowers of one sex. Catkins are found only on woody plants.

Compound leaves. Leaves in which the blade is composed of 2 or more parts that look like separate leaves and are called *leaflets.*

Corm. A fleshy, vertical enlargement of the part of the stem that occurs below the surface of the ground. It looks like a bulb but is solid and not composed of layers as are bulbs.

Disk flowers. The tubular flowers located at the center of the flower heads of typical members of the Composite family. In members of this family, what looks like a single flower is often 2 types of flowers: a dense central cluster of *disk flowers,* which is ringed by rows of *ray flowers* that look like petals. Some species have flower heads composed of a single type.

Family. In botany, a grouping of plants consisting of a number of related *genera.*

Fruit. The seeds of a plant and their enclosure. Includes berries, nuts, and grains.

Genus. A subdivision of a *family* composed of a group of closely related *species.*

Grain. Fruits peculiar to members of the grass family. They are small and dry and contain a single seed.

Habitat. The environment in which a plant is usually found growing.

Head. A dense cluster of flowers in which the individual flowers lack stalks and rise from the flattened top of a stem. Usually refers to the blossoms of members of the Composite family (*e.g.,* the Sunflower).

Herb. A plant with soft, nonwoody stems in which the parts above ground die back at the end of each growing season.

Leaflet. The small, leaf-like subdivisions of a *compound leaf.*

Leafstalk. The part of the leaf that connects the *blade* to the stem.

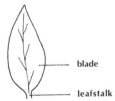

Lobe. Sections of a leaf formed by the indentation of edges.

Nut. A fruit with a hard stony or woody shell surrounding the seed.

Opposite. Refers to leaves and other plant parts that occur in pairs on the stems.

Palmately compound. A *compound leaf* in which the *leaflets* are all attached to the end of the leaf stalk.

Perennial. A plant that lives from year to year and does not die after flowering.

Petal. One of the inner parts of a flower and a part that is usually colored (see diagram, p. 224).

Pinnately compound. A *compound leaf* in which the *leaflets* are arranged along a central stalk like feathers on a bird's wing.

Pistil. The organ in the center of a flower that contains the female reproductive system (see diagram, p. 224).

Pith. Soft, spongy tissue filling the center of stems. It is usually white.

Ray flower. The outer rows of flowers in the flower heads of the Composite family. They are flattened, look like petals, and ring the *disk flowers.*

Rhizome. A horizontal underground stem of *perennial* plants that is often confused with a root. It differs from roots in having buds and/or leaf scars along its length. Rhizomes are sometimes thick and fleshy and act as storage organs for starch.

Rosette. A cluster of *basal* leaves flattened against the ground.

Sepal. A segment of the *calyx* of a flower, usually green and located just outside the petals (see diagram, p. 224).

Serrate. Fine teeth with points that are angled toward the tip of a leaf.

Shoot. A young branch or stem.

Shrub. A relatively small woody plant with major branches

that originate at ground level rather than from a single trunk.

Species. The most basic unit of classification. A number of closely related species form a *genus.*

Spike. A finger-shaped flower cluster in which the individual flowers attach directly and lack stalks.

Stamen. The pollen-producing or male organs of flowers. They are usually arranged around the *pistil* (see diagram).

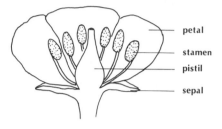

Taproot. A stout vertical root that supports smaller lateral branches. Dandelions have this type of root as do carrots.

Tuber. A swollen enlargement on a root or rhizome often occurring some distance from the above-ground parts of the plant. Potatoes are tubers.

Umbel. A type of flower cluster in which the stalks of the individual flowers rise from a common point. It resembles an umbrella that has been turned inside out.

Vein. A bundle of dense tissue that acts as the support and conducting system for nutrients in leaves.

Whorl. A cluster of 3 or more leaves that are attached to the stem at the same level or a cluster of flowers that surrounds the stem at places where leaves are attached.

Index